Cataloging-in-Publication Data has been applied for and may be obtained
from the Library of Congress.

ISBN 978-1-4197-3187-7

Printed and bound in China
10 9 8 7 6 5 4 3

Abrams Books for Young Readers are available at special discounts when
purchased in quantity for premiums and promotions as well as fundraising
or educational use. Special editions can also be created to specification. For
details, contact specialsales@abramsbooks.com or the address below.

Abrams® is a registered trademark of Harry N. Abrams, Inc.

ABRAMS The Art of Books
195 Broadway, New York, NY 10007
abramsbooks.com

TO MY TWO BOYS,
WHO WILL ONE DAY READ
THIS AND BECOME
MEMORIZING SUPERHEROES!
— N.D.

TO KATHI AND SCOTT,
FOR ALWAYS BELIEVING
IN MY SUPERPOWER
— S.S.

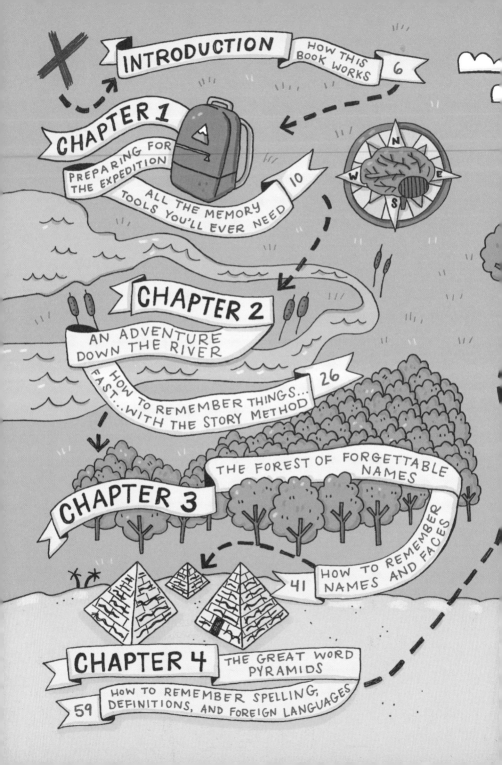

INTRODUCTION
How This Book Works

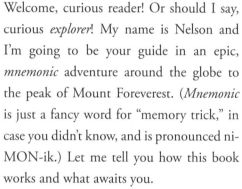

HI!

Welcome, curious reader! Or should I say, curious *explorer*! My name is Nelson and I'm going to be your guide in an epic, *mnemonic* adventure around the globe to the peak of Mount Foreverest. (*Mnemonic* is just a fancy word for "memory trick," in case you didn't know, and is pronounced ni-MON-ik.) Let me tell you how this book works and what awaits you.

In these pages are some seriously crazy exploits that I will ask you to imagine. Each chapter will tell a story that is part of your fantastical journey, but along the way, I'll also be teaching you memory techniques and skills, some of which are thousands of years old. I want to challenge your memory and brain to do some exciting, and occasionally difficult, tasks. But don't worry, I'll make it as fun and easy as possible.

As your guide on our globe-trotting exploit, I will teach you the secret, long-forgotten practices of memorization with the ultimate goal of reaching the summit of Mount Foreverest—the mountain of remembering forever. And the best part? These techniques will help make learning and studying much easier. It will be like having your own memory superpowers! Imagine being able to remember more—like names and faces, lists of things, numbers, and important dates—but with less work. Think of all the free time you will have to go on other adventures with your friends!

Why Mount Foreverest? you may be asking. Well, my goal is to head to the top of that summit so we can confront and defeat the Memory Thief. It is high on that mountain where he recently began to rule, and it's a mysterious place where few have gone. Since arriving there not too long ago, his powers have become so great that he's able to steal memories from anyone and everyone when they're not looking! I have decided to stop him once and for all. But I can't do it alone; he's too powerful. I'll need your help. And if we don't stop him, more and more people will lose their ability to remember things.

Maybe you're a bit skeptical about this so-called Memory Thief. I bet you're thinking, *Does he even exist?* and *Can he really steal our memories?* Let me answer that by asking *you* a question:

What did you have for dinner five days ago?

You can't remember, can you? And think of all those *other* things you don't remember or the things you've forgotten over the years. That's him—the Memory Thief—hard at work on his evil plans to plunder our memories. But I have a plan to stop him and save all the memories in the world so that people will be able to remember whatever they want, *forever*! But I need your help. Will you join me on this adventure? I would be incredibly grateful. Please oh please? Don't take too long to answer; time is running out.

You will? Oh, thank goodness! Everyone I've asked so far has turned me down, telling me they're too scared to face the Memory Thief. The only requirement I have for you is that you have a good memory.

Oh, you don't think you have one? Not to worry! Part of my plan is to train you along the way. You're smart and I can tell you've got guts, so you'll pick up these techniques in *no time*!

Here's the plan:

To get to the Memory Thief, we'll have to scale the summit of Foreverest, and get past some rather tall gates, which are locked. That scheming villain, however, has broken the key to the gates into three pieces and scattered them around the world, so we'll need to find them first. To secure each piece, we'll have to pass some short memory tests, but I'll do my best to prepare you in advance.

One more thing.

No matter how silly, weird, or strange our journey gets, you have to promise me that you will do what I ask of you . . . no matter what! It's the only way we'll succeed in getting all the pieces of the key. So, whether I ask you to recall a hilarious

image in your mind so you can pass a ferocious yeti guard at the foot of the Himalayas, or to answer bizarre questions from a pirate in order to open up his secret treasure chest, you *have* to do it. Promise? The fate of human memory depends on it!

With all of that out of the way, let us begin our journey . . .

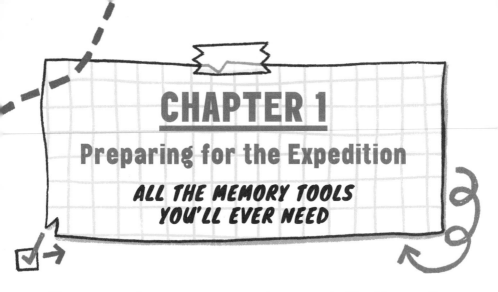

CHAPTER 1
Preparing for the Expedition
ALL THE MEMORY TOOLS YOU'LL EVER NEED

Chances are you've never gone on an adventure quite like this, so we'll make sure that you're well equipped. That means knowing all the necessary things you need to bring along, but maybe more important is knowing what to leave behind. Our adventure is going to be long and hard, so we must get rid of unhelpful concepts that will slow us down. Mostly, these are ideas you may already have about memory that you think are okay but are *actually* wrong. They need to be thrown out immediately so you stand a chance on Mount Foreverest!

NELSON'S THREE THINGS TO FORGET AND LEAVE AT HOME

● **Some people are born with horrible memories.**

I hear this one all the time. Many people think that a bad memory is something you're either born with or you're not. They believe that if you're lucky enough to have been gifted with a *good* memory at birth then you're awesome and live a charmed life where studying is easy, and you pass all your tests without much effort. And they think that if you have a *bad* memory, you're doomed to a life where studying is really hard and that you won't do well in school.

Well, here's the good news: That is totally and completely, flat-out WRONG! A bad memory is not something you're born with. In fact, we all have the same basic abilities. And while some people might have better natural memories than others, the good news is that *bad* memory can *always* be trained into a good one.

Don't believe me? Well, when I was your age, my memory was not so great—actually I'd even say it was probably even worse than that of the average person. I was horrible at memorizing things. My teacher would assign homework that involved remembering lists and facts, and I would hate it. I struggled so much, and just trying would take me for-*ev*-errr! And to make matters worse, the next day at school, I would be so nervous about forgetting things that I actually did forget things, just like I had feared. I would turn red in front of the entire class and a lot of the kids would laugh at me! Ugh. I can't think of a worse feeling.

But a few years ago, when I heard about these strange things called *mnemonics*, I decided to learn all about them and practiced the techniques every day. Before long, I was crowned the USA Memory Champion!

Did you know such a competition existed? Don't worry, most people don't. It's an event where contestants memorize all sorts of things as fast and as accurately as possible on the spot. When I won it

for the first time, I was named the best memorizer in the country! Not only that, but I could memorize some really impressive things: a whole deck of randomly shuffled playing cards in under a minute, a roomful of people's names, even a number that was four hundred digits long. Crazy, right? I went from having a horrible memory to having the *best* memory in the country in only a few months. I even set some national records along the way and then ended up winning the USA Memory Championship three more times after that. But here's the crazier part:

You can do all of those things, too! All it takes is for someone like me to show you the ropes and reveal the way to memory awesomeness. Together, we'll defeat the Memory Thief and help everyone remember whatever they want to!

So there. If you've ever said to yourself, *OOOF! My memory is horrrrrible!* STOP. Don't say that anymore. Throw those negative feelings into the garbage right now! Memory is a skill that you can improve just like playing the piano, ice-skating, or painting (and is actually probably easier to do than all of those other things). *No one* has a bad memory—NO ONE. Just remind yourself of that if you ever get frustrated. Repeat the phrase "I have an unforgettable memory!" if you ever have doubt.

● Your brain can fill up.

Do you ever feel like your brain can hold only so many things at once? Or when you're studying, does it seem like there's just too much information already stored in your brain and you couldn't possibly cram one more single piece of information in there?

Well, you'll have to leave behind that idea, too, because get this: The brain is nearly unlimited in what it can hold.

That's right. You heard me—*unlimited.*

Sounds a bit ridiculous, but it's true. Unfortunately, most people see the brain as containing a finite amount of storage space . . . like a parking garage that can just hold a very specific number of cars and no more. And if a few cars exit, then—and *only* then—can some new cars enter. Your brain is *not* like that at all. Your brain is made up of millions of connections between things called neurons. It's more similar to something like a spiderweb, where all things are connected. And the more you add to it, the larger the web grows and the stronger it becomes.

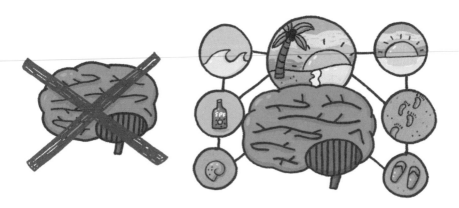

Let me show you an example: Try to think of a memory in your own life from the last year . . . summer vacation, Thanksgiving, your birthday—any one of those will do. Now try to remember a *specific* memory from that time and mull it over for a few seconds. You'll probably start thinking about a small detail, maybe what you were wearing, what your parents said to you, what the weather was like, some really funny thing that happened, etc. But the more you ponder it, the more you'll find your mind jumping to *other* memories that the first memory reminded you of. Maybe that really funny thing that happened reminds you of a cartoon you once watched. Then *that* new memory will lead you to *another* one, and before you know it, you're thinking about something totally different from that first memory you started with. Why? Because all of your memories are connected. One is connected to the next, is connected to the next, is connected to the next . . .

The bottom line is that your memory can never get full. It can only get stronger and better connected. So don't ever feel like you're running out of space in your memory. You can *always* add more things to that web!

14

yawwwn

Memorizing is boring and hard.

Nope, nope, nope. The only reason anyone thinks memorizing is boring or hard is because no one has ever taught them the fun and easy way. Simple as that. Chances are, most times that you've had to memorize something, you went about it by repeating it over and over again (yawn!). That's called "rote" memorization and, yep, that *is* boring, hard, and definitely not fun. Rote memorization is about as enjoyable as reading the back of a shampoo bottle.

Don't worry, it's not your fault. The real problem is that no one has ever taught you the *right* way to use your memory. Fret not! We won't be doing any boring stuff on our adventures. We'll be learning the *right* way to use our memories. In other words: fun, fun, fun!

I'll even make a deal with you. I promise that on our adventures, I will *only* have you memorize things in a fun and exciting way. If I ever break that promise, you have every right to take this book and flush it down the toilet. (Just don't tell your parents, and do it in clumps of pages at a time so you don't have to call the plumber.) Just kidding—maybe just put the book back on the shelf and forget you ever read it.

Memorizing can and *should always be* fun and easy. Never forget that!

What to Bring

Now that you have a good idea of what to leave behind on our adventure, let me tell you the important things you *must* bring. Because the challenges ahead will involve us using our mind and memory to the max, the main part of our expedition gear will be made up of things called *mind tools*. There are three of them that I'll be giving you and they are the basic tools to help you remember absolutely anything and to defeat the Memory Thief. But just like any tools, if you don't use them enough (or correctly), they'll get rusty and won't work! So make sure to use them often and you should be fine.

NELSON'S THREE MIND TOOLS

This first tool is all about **SEE**ing **IT AS A PICTURE IN YOUR MIND**. We have the amazing power of somehow being able to see things using our *imagination*. For example, if I asked you to *imagine* a slice of pizza, you could see a picture of that slice in your mind, right? Maybe you're picturing it on a plate in the kitchen, waiting to be eaten, or maybe you're imagining a rotten, stinky slice you've thrown against the school bus window because you're angry at your mom for packing the wrong lunch. Well, what if I asked you to give this pizza slice a pair of roller skates to wear? Now the slice is doing pirouettes in the kitchen (or down the aisle of the bus). How about now giving the slice a pair of sunglasses, a crazy green and blue hairstyle, and making it whistle "Jingle Bells"? Bizarre, right?

What's great about **SEE**ing is the fact that we can **SEE** *anything* we want in our minds. No matter how outrageous it is, our mind's imagination can always bend backward and see the impossible. That's what makes this so fun, too!

So no matter what you have to memorize, try to **SEE** it as a picture in your mind. Sometimes that's easy to do (like with that silly slice of pizza), but other times it may seem tricky. (How do you come up with a silly image for a long number, for example?) But don't worry, stuff like that is not so hard. I'll show you how to **SEE** them in later chapters.

Once you've found a way to **SEE** what you are memorizing, the next step is to **LINK** it to **SOMETHING THAT YOU ALREADY KNOW**. The problem with most people's memories is that they don't put the things they want to remember in places that are easy to find later on when they need to recall them.

Huh?

Think of it like this: You've saved a file on your computer before, haven't you? What usually happens? You click the SAVE button, right? And then what happens? A little box pops up and asks you to give your newly created file a name, and then you need to tell the computer in which folder you want it be stored ("Documents" or "Nelson's Awesome Memory Techniques," for example). We do this because the clever folks who invented computers wanted you to have an easy way to find that file later on. (You know it's a document, so it's probably stored in your "Documents" folder, under the filename you gave it—voilà, you've found it!) Now imagine that computers didn't work like that—that instead, when you clicked SAVE, no box popped up at all and the file you saved is in some random place inside the computer. Yikes! How would you ever find it again? Probably never! And your computer would be a downright mess.

I hate to say it, but that messy computer is what your brain is like, too. When you try to memorize things, you're not "saving" them correctly. That's what the **LINK** tool is all about. Taking your mental picture from **SEE** and saving it correctly to your brain's mental hard drive. Thinking about how to do that exactly may seem a bit weird or might even sound impossible, but it's actually quite easy to master with just a bit of practice.

Now, what does **LINK**ing actually mean? And how do we do it?

Think of something you know. What's the name of the street you live on? Or what's the third letter of the alphabet? Or when is your birthday? There are things you know like the back of your hand, which can be used to **LINK** new information. Actually, your brain does this a lot already. Whenever your teacher is teaching you something new, they might compare it to something else you already know to help you understand it. For example, let's pretend that the only animal you know of is a dog and your teacher is trying to explain to you what a bird is. (I know you know what a bird is, but let's just pretend!)

Your teacher might say, "A bird is like a dog, only smaller, with wings and feathers, with a beak instead of teeth, and can fly." BAM! Now you know what a bird is. You've managed to use that superpowerful spiderweb of brain neurons to **LINK** a "bird" to that familiar "dog."

There are many different ways to use the **LINK** tool for storing pictures in our head, but that's what our adventure is for: learning all those different brain hacks as we navigate to the summit of Mount Foreverest and face the Memory Thief.

Okay, at this point you've taken what you wanted to memorize and found a way to **SEE** it and **LINK** it—now you need to take that final tool, the **GO!** tool, and get all of it spinning together. Let me explain what that means.

If you need to memorize something quickly, coming up with pictures (**SEE**ing) and placing them in a location (**LINK**ing) will do the trick for a little bit, but if you *really* want to make something unforgettable you need to **GO!** Think of the **GO!** tool as the final step in which you mesh and glue everything all together and add that extra magic bizarre sauce that makes a memory stick like the strongest superglue you've ever used!

NOTE TO READER

For some reason, bizarre things are really, really hard to forget. It's actually almost like superglue for our memories. The sillier, weirder, colorful-ier, noisier, and bizarre-ier you can make that picture, the stickier it becomes and the harder it is to forget.

Here's how you use it: Take what you have from **SEE** and take what you have from **LINK** and smash them together as one. In other words, take the mental picture you have in your head for what you're memorizing and **LINK** it to the thing you already know. Imagine them connected somehow. Things don't stick unless you add glue or tape or gum, right? So that's what the **GO!** tool does. And the way to make that glue really sticky in our brain is by using at least two (or more) of the following things:

☑ **SENSES** —Use sight, touch, smell, hearing, and/or taste.

☑ **LAUGH OUT LOUD** —Have it make you laugh out loud!

☑ **EXAGGERATION** —Make it bigger, longer, smaller, smellier, uglier.

☑ **WEIRDNESS** —Make it so ridiculously weird.

☑ **OPPOSITE** —Flip it around. If it's forward, make it backward. If it's big, make it small.

☑ **MOVEMENT** —Give it an action. Have it do something.

☑ **GROSSNESS** —Have it make you go, Ewwww!

Let's go back to that slice of pizza from before. To make that slice super sticky in your head, you're going to have to turn all the dials up to 11 and imagine the most insane pizza-related scene possible. We already made it pretty weird by giving the slice some roller skates, a crazy hairstyle, and a tune to whistle, but let's go even further. Let's try using our senses more. That means the cheese on the pizza is bubbling and sizzling and it's making crazy gurgling noises (there's your sound). The grease is dripping

off of it and scalding your hands (there's the touch/feel). Better yet, your hands are on fire because it's so hot. ARGHH! Or maybe it doesn't smell and taste like pizza—maybe it's more like dog poop (smell). YUCK!

In the end, the important thing is to make it MEMORABLE. The more you build your mental picture into something with all your senses and that weirdness overload, the more those mind tools will kick into gear and the more your memories will start to stick!

So basically, all I'm asking you to do with this third tool is just think of the weirdest, silliest thing you can come up with that moves, uses your senses, and makes you laugh. Sounds easy, doesn't it? Well, that's because it is. And just you wait and see when we start on our journey—it's going to be a blast!

A Few More Things to Bring

All right, you're almost all packed and ready to go. Here are a few last-minute items I need you to put in your mental rucksack before we head out the door to scale Mount Foreverest. These aren't as important and powerful as the mind tools themselves, but they will help them work more smoothly if you know them.

 TRUST

Trust your memory! It sounds easy enough, but it's the key to improving and getting better at memorizing. Your memory *hates* not being trusted. If it ever feels like you don't trust it, it will fight back and make you forget something. (Your memory can be a jerk sometimes!) But if you have *confidence* in your memory and you really believe in it, you'll be amazed at how powerful those mind tools can be!

☑ ATTENTION AND FOCUS

Memorization can only happen if you are paying attention to something. If you're off in Never-Never Land while someone is trying to explain something to you, you're never going to remember it, no matter how many mind tools you use! So always be in the moment, paying attention to the thing you want to memorize. I know it's hard to do that sometimes, especially since there are so many distractions in the world. But one thing I do when I know I'm going to be distracted is to remove the distractions on purpose before they become a problem. That means switching off the TV before I study or putting my phone in my pocket when someone is talking to me. And even if you fail sometimes at making something stick, no worries. Back up and try again. Don't forget that memory is a skill, and like any skill, to really get good at it, you need to practice. I didn't become a big-time memory champion overnight; it took some time.

☑ A SENSE OF FUN!

Lastly (and I can't stress this enough!), HAVE FUN! Memorizing is fun and silly and makes you feel like you have a superpower. It's the greatest skill you'll ever learn. Have fun with it!

Are you ready to do this?

Without further ado, let's get started on this adventure. Grab your **SEE-LINK-GO!** tools and all your other memory tidbits I told you to pack and follow me out the door to the first part of our adventure and into the world of mnemonics!

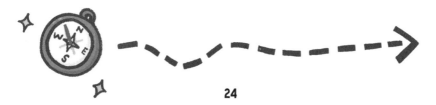

CHAPTER 2
An Adventure Down the River
HOW TO REMEMBER LISTS OF THINGS . . . FAST . . . WITH THE STORY METHOD

With any adventure, it always starts by taking one step out the door. Let's start our journey to Mount Foreverest, shall we?

Out the door we go and straight down the . . . Wait, what's this? We suddenly walk smack into a large—and I mean *ginormous*—washing machine. It's huge, towering above you as it vibrates from all the spinning going on inside of it. You peer upward at the giant structure until your neck can't bend anymore. It's taller than any building you've ever seen! What on earth is it doing here making all this noise and spinning at a million miles an hour?

You look through the window of the washing machine's door and notice something even stranger: Not only is it a WASHING MACHINE, but it's filled with a TON of bright red APPLES spinning furiously.

Who puts apples in their washing machine? you think to yourself.

You barely have a moment to wonder about it any further before a chubby CHEF, dressed in a big white hat and a long food-stained apron, asks us to move out of the way and manages to pry open the massive washing machine door (with a *lot* of effort, mind you).

"Out of the way! I've got a pie to make!" he shouts at us as the deluge of apples and water pour out of the machine overhead. We're instantly drenched and wiping water from our eyes, when suddenly, what weirdness do we see before us but that very same chef now dressed in a costume like the MAD HATTER. Huh? Gosh, that's strange. Not only that, but we see him run down the street toward the nearby river, where he jumps in a rowboat and starts to row. He is now a MAN ROWING.

We've got to follow him! The first leg of our expedition just so happens to be down the same river he took off on, so let's go!

We find a skiff on the edge of the river, hop aboard, and start paddling our way downstream, where eventually the current carries us. After a half hour or so, we're well on our way down this river and on an adventure! We've lost sight of the chef/Mad Hatter by now, but not to worry, there's only one way to go, and that's in the direction of the dam we can start to make out in the distance.

As we near the dam, you start to notice some rapidly moving object at the top of it. You nudge me and point to the dam. SQUINTING at the DAM to see what you're pointing at, I suddenly see what it is: It's a JACKHAMMER, jackhammering into the top of the dam trying to . . . Uh-oh! Trying to crack the dam open! Gagh!

We better pick up the pace or that dam is going to burst open and sink our tiny boat. Just in the nick of time, a VAN, BURNING, flies out from the riverbank and lands—SPLASH—into the river, right next to us. Who cares that it's burning, the driver is none other than a HAIRY SUN, shining bright yellow, and sporting a thick beard. Weird!

"Get in," he yells at us.

This hairy sun is pretty bright and intimidating, so we're not going to turn him down, burning van or not. Plus, the dam ahead of us is just about to blow—maybe he can help. As we jump into the floating van, suddenly a NECKTIE appears from nowhere, floats over to the jackhammer, and ties a knot around it so it can no longer do any jackhammering.

"Guys, see that small opening in the crack in the dam ahead?" the hairy sun asks us.

We nod. Part way down the massive crack, we see a slight opening where some water is seeping through. Not only that but there is something

POKING out of it. It's a TAIL, wagging furiously. Oh no! There must be an animal stuck in there!

We look at each other and agree that we have to save the animal, no matter how dangerous the situation looks. We get the van floating toward the dam, and when at the base, I decide to start climbing up the steep wall to the opening.

"I'm going up! Grab the camera and make sure to film me!" I shout down to you.

No sooner do you take the role of FILMER for this heroic act, the camera overheats and explodes (talk about bad luck, eh?). Pieces of shrapnel from the camera fly everywhere and PIERCE the back of a CANNON lying off to the side of the dam. In an unfortunate chain of events, it lights the fuse of the cannon, causing it to fire and launch a bunch of book-shaped cannonballs—BOOM!—at the dam (it's a BOOK-CANNON). This dam was already so close to crumbling in the first place, but those books were just enough to finish the job.

A slow rumble starts to grow as the whole dam begins to shake more and more vigorously until . . . KAPLOW! The whole thing breaks open and we're catapulted into the air. Luckily, we all land safely on some pieces of driftwood that were heading downstream: you, me, the hairy sun, and the rescued dog that's now happily wagging his tail. After a few minutes of drifting downstream and catching our breath, we paddle to shore to pitch our camp for the night.

That's enough craziness for the day, don't you think? And it's getting dark, so we better start a fire and get all of our gear dry. We pitch our tents, cook ourselves some food, and then crawl into our sleeping bags for a bit of well-earned rest. Tomorrow's a big day! We'll finish the route down the river and reach our first objective: the Forest of Forgettable Names.

The next morning, we wake up nice and early and start our way down the river again, alone, leaving our friends behind. Following the last few curves of the riverbank, we finally reach the entrance to the Forest of Forgettable Names, and hear a loud blaring of trumpets—*Dun, da-da, dunnnnnn!*

We have arrived.

Now, before we continue any further, let's take a moment to quickly review everything that just happened to us, from start to finish. This is *very* important! I know for a *fact* that whoever tries to enter the forest, there is an elf guarding the entrance who will quiz you on things that

have just happened to you. Hopefully with your help, we'll be able to remember everything. We *have* to get inside the forest. Deep inside lies the first piece of the key to the summit of Mount Foreverest!

Do you remember everything that just happened to us? If not, we'll do a quick recap in just a moment. But first, I wanted to reveal to you our first memory lesson, which I've already secretly taught you.

Remember in the last chapter when I mentioned there were a few ways to use that **LINK** tool? Well, guess what? We've just used one of the ways.

The method we used in this chapter was something called **THE STORY METHOD**. The way it works is, you take all the images you create from your **SEE** tool, then you connect them all in a story, where one picture connects—or **LINK**s—to the next, and the next one connects to the next, and so on, creating a long chain of images. You've seen a chain before, right? How each metal loop links into the next one, and the next one into the one after that? That's what we're doing, but with our mental images.

Now, **THE STORY METHOD** isn't the *only* way to store a bunch of images, but it is one of the quickest and easiest ways. Whenever you want to recall your list, all you have to do is start at the very beginning of your story and move from image to image until you reach the end. That's it! The story keeps everything nicely connected and in order. It's super easy.

Think of our river adventure. What did we start with? A big WASHING MACHINE with a TON of things inside it, right? That's our first image, and then that image linked to the APPLES, and then that linked to the CHEF, then MAD HATTER, then MAN ROWING, and so on. Catch my drift?

Pause for a moment, close your eyes, and see if you can remember the rest of the story, all the way to the last image (which was BOOK-CANNON). If you have a few blanks, no worries. Just try again. Most of it should be in your memory!

THE STORY METHOD works amazingly for memorizing lists of things . . . Maybe something, perhaps, like all of the U.S. presidents? Here's another surprise for you: The river adventure we just went on? It helped us already memorize the first fifteen! Can you believe that?

You don't? Well, check this out. Here's the list of key points from our story to help it all make more sense.

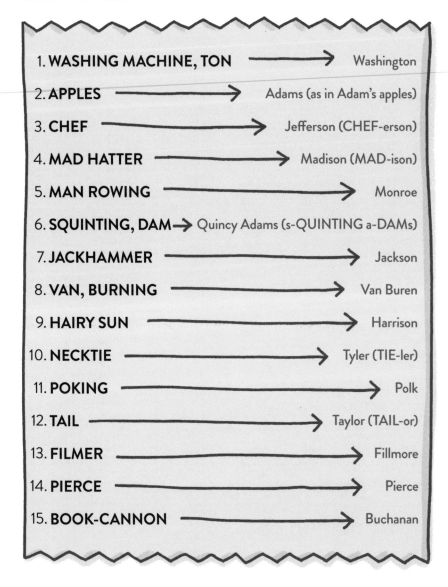

1. **WASHING MACHINE, TON** ──────→ Washington

2. **APPLES** ──────→ Adams (as in Adam's apples)

3. **CHEF** ──────→ Jefferson (CHEF-erson)

4. **MAD HATTER** ──────→ Madison (MAD-ison)

5. **MAN ROWING** ──────→ Monroe

6. **SQUINTING, DAM** → Quincy Adams (s-QUINTING a-DAMs)

7. **JACKHAMMER** ──────→ Jackson

8. **VAN, BURNING** ──────→ Van Buren

9. **HAIRY SUN** ──────→ Harrison

10. **NECKTIE** ──────→ Tyler (TIE-ler)

11. **POKING** ──────→ Polk

12. **TAIL** ──────→ Taylor (TAIL-or)

13. **FILMER** ──────→ Fillmore

14. **PIERCE** ──────→ Pierce

15. **BOOK-CANNON** ──────→ Buchanan

If you'd like to learn the complete story so you know all forty-five presidents, check out the Appendix for more details.

NOTE TO READER

All of those bold keywords I asked you to pay attention to were funny images to help you remember the names of the first fifteen U.S. presidents! Notice that the words we remembered were not exactly the same as the name of the president, but close enough to help us get a clue as to what the real name is.

I won't always be there to come up with the images for you like I did on this river adventure, so when you're trying to **SEE** an image on your own, for whatever you're trying to memorize, try to use whatever comes to your mind first. That's usually going to be the strongest image. Maybe it sounds like some other word, or maybe it reminds you of someone or something. Go with that! **LINK** it to the next image, and don't forget, you also have to **GO!** with it. If it's a bit strange or odd, even better. Just **GO!** for it.

Ta-da! Easy as pie. Everything that has happened to us so far has been really silly, I know, but go back and try to remember it all and really try and visualize the story in your mind this time! It's easy to remember, fun, and already preloaded with all the **SEE-LINK-GO!** tool action that we need to make it memorable! I guarantee that if you close your eyes and try to retell the story, you'll see that you already have the entire story memorized. Amazing, isn't it? It's incredible how easily our brains eat up those story-based, bizarre kinds of things.

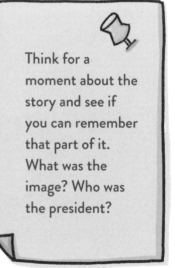

WELCOME!

Next on our journey, we march up to a vast expanse of towering trees and are greeted by an elf guard.

"Welcome, adventurers! You have reached the Forest of Forgettable Names! If you'd like to advance any further, I'm going to have to ask you a few questions about your trip getting here. You see, I'm not like some ordinary elf; I can see into your past. So I know all that has happened to you on the river. Remember incorrectly and you will have to go back from whence you came!"

Gulp. You ready? You can do this . . .

"Okay, first question is for you, Nelson," the elf starts. "What was wagging in the crack of the dam? And what was the name of the president linked to that image?"

"Hmm . . . a TAIL! . . . and, um . . . er . . . TAYLOR was the president!" I reply.

"That is correct! Question number two is for you, young reader! What did the chef dress in after you first saw him? And what was the name of the president linked to *that* image?"

"A Mad Hatter costume, you say? That is correct! And Madison? Yup, you got it! One last question for the both of you and I shall let

Think for a moment about the story and see if you can remember that part of it. What was the image? Who was the president?

38

you pass . . . What object landed with a big splash in the river? And what president was that?"

We look at each other, nod, and in unison shout, "A VAN, BURNING! PRESIDENT VAN BUREN!"

And with that, the thicket of trees suddenly opens up just wide enough to allow the two of us through. We give each other a high five, thank the elf guard, and enter into the Forest of Forgettable Names.

On to the next challenge!

Great job so far. You've just learned one of the best skills for learning lists of things. If you just recall our recent river adventure, you should be able to say the first fifteen presidents in perfect order! **THE STORY METHOD** is great for situations where you need to memorize a list of things very quickly without much preparation. It's great for remembering to-do lists, grocery lists, instructions from your teacher, lists of facts, and so on. So, from now on, if you ever need to memorize a list, just **SEE** all the things you need to memorize as pictures and **LINK** them all together using **THE STORY METHOD** (create a well-connected story). And of course, don't forget to **GO!**

Take a blank sheet of paper and ask one of your family members (or a friend!) to write down ten random words. Then, try using **THE STORY METHOD** to memorize those words in order, just like we did in this chapter.

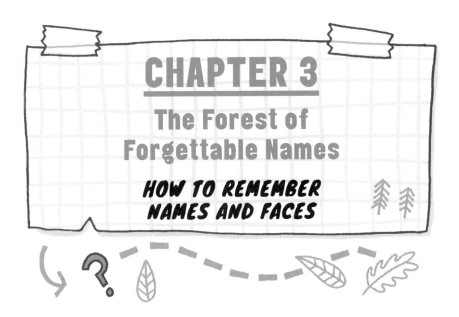

CHAPTER 3

The Forest of Forgettable Names

HOW TO REMEMBER NAMES AND FACES

By now, you've gotten a feel for just how strange this journey is going to be—anything you can imagine is fair game! And it's fun, right? I know the ride down the river was a bit hectic at times, getting us soaking wet, tossing us about, and seeing some really weird stuff, but in the end, we got through it *and* we learned something pretty neat without really thinking about it: the first fifteen U.S. presidents!

Now, as we make our way through this forest, let me warn you about what's to come. I've heard a lot about what happens in here and what will be needed to get our hands on that first piece of the key.

First of all, there's a reason why this forest is called the Forest of Forgettable Names. All of the elves who live here have names, but unfortunately, they're all really unusual ones—so unusual that no one can even remember them! What's worse, the elves can't even remember their *own* names. All of them have to carry an ID card in their pocket with their name on it so they can check it when they need to. Yikes!

I'm telling you all this because, in a little while, we'll come across a very tall tree with a narrow circular stairway inside it that winds all the way to the top. Up there, we'll find the King of the Forgettable Name Forest, who's the most forgetful elf of them all. He holds the first piece to the key, but he's forgotten what it's for so he keeps it protected hoping that one day he will remember. He's also lost his ID card, so he has no idea what his name is. If we can somehow help him remember it, and help him remember all the names of his family members (who also live in the tree with him), I have a feeling that he'll be so pleased with us, and that he'll give us anything we want—including that fragment of the key!

We've still got a little while before we arrive there so I'm going to explain to you how to use **SEE-LINK-GO!** to remember any name you want so you'll be ready when we get there.

Everywhere I go, I always hear people say, "I'm terrible at remembering names!" Maybe you've said something like that before, too? The truth is, people just haven't learned how to go about it correctly. (Also, we know the Memory Thief is hard at work making you forget things, so he's partly to blame as well.)

The first tip I'm going to give you for remembering names is really, really simple:

Try a little harder.

Seriously, just try. Most people are simply too busy, lazy, or nervous to try. Maybe they're thinking of something else when they meet someone or maybe they didn't hear the person's name properly and are too embarrassed to ask for it again. But if you stop for a second and try to focus on hearing and remembering the name or just ask their name one more time, I bet you all the dollars in the world that you'll instantly be better at it. Maybe not perfect, but it's a start!

Next time you go to class or hang out with a group of people you don't know, try to remember as many names as you can just by trying to focus. Make it a game! Tell yourself, *Okay, I'm going to memorize ten names* (or any number of names you feel comfortable with) in this group of people. You'll be surprised at how well you do just by making the effort!

Why do we forget names so easily? And why do they seem so hard to remember? It's simple. Think of it like this: Do you speak French? No, probably not. So, if I said the word *chien*, would you know what that meant? Would you be able to remember it? Maybe . . . but probably not for very long. The reason is because it's a word that doesn't mean anything to you because you don't speak French, duh! (Unless you *do*, in which case this was a bad example.) Names are sort of their own language of weird, foreign words. When you meet a person, they tell you that strange word that is their name and you're expected to remember it. But like French words, the word doesn't mean anything to you, so you will eventually forget it. Names don't stick well.

I think you see where I'm going . . . If we can apply the **SEE-LINK-GO!** process to any name we hear, we'd be giving it a picture (that's the **SEE** part), attaching it to something we already know (that's the **LINK** part), and then **GO!**-ing with it, to really make that picture explode onto your brain pan. All of that together is going to turn any name from an incomprehensible foreign word into an easy-to-digest English word. In other words, something that makes sense to you and which is MEMORABLE!

I can see you nodding your head, but I still see a bit of confusion. You understand **SEE-LINK-GO!** but how do you use it specifically for names?

Oh, look! I can see the tall tree we've been searching for just ahead. There should be a guard there waiting to guide us up the winding staircase. Let's make sure to ask him for his name so we can practice before we meet the king.

As we walk up to the base of the tree, a cheery elf with a big, red, scraggly beard pops out of a little wooden guardhouse just beside the entrance to the staircase.

"Hello, friends, my name is . . ." The elf digs through his pockets to find his ID card and pulls it out, reading, "Wickley. Ah yes, my name is Wickley. How can I help you?"

"Thanks, Wickley," I reply. "We're here to see the king. We are memory experts and can help him remember his name!"

"Oh wow! That would be very helpful, indeed! He lost his ID card decades ago and no one knows what his name is. Calling him by his real name would sure beat having to keep calling him 'dude' or 'guy.' He hates that!" the guard says as he begins leading us up the stairs. "Right this way!"

All right, we're in business! While we make this journey upward—and to get a little practice—let's figure out how to remember this guard's name. To do that, let me show you how **SEE-LINK-GO!** works for memorizing names.

Okay, **SEE** the name as a mental picture. Here are a few ideas for what you can do to quickly turn it into a picture:

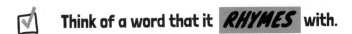

Think of a word that it **RHYMES** with.

Think of a word that it **REMINDS** you of (maybe it looks or sounds like another word you know).

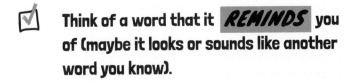

Think of a person you already know with the **SAME NAME** (it could be a friend, someone in your family, or even your favorite cartoon character).

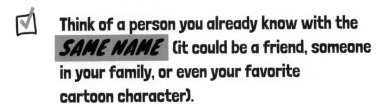

If the name is long, or you've thought about it and still can't come up with a picture, break the name into smaller syllables and try again for each syllable.

Here are a few examples, just to give you a taste:

STEVE—*Stove* // Steve almost looks the same as *stove*. A *stove* is easy to picture!

BOB—*Bobby pin* // Bob reminds me of the start of the word *bobby pin*.

JEN—*Pen* // Jen and *pen* rhyme with each other.

NELSON—Oof, that's a tough one! Let me break it into smaller words: **Nel**—*Nail* // Nel and *nail* sound pretty close! **Son**—*Sun* // They sound exactly the same! Since we have two words here, let's smoosh them together. Imagine a *nail* being hammered into the bright *sun*. *Nail-sun* = NELSON!

If you're thinking, *Nelson, these pictures have nothing to do with the name*, well . . . you're right. And that's okay! Remember, the name is hard to remember, so if we can think of a word that's *easier* for you to remember instead of the name, it's going to make the process of **SEE-LINK-GO!** much easier.

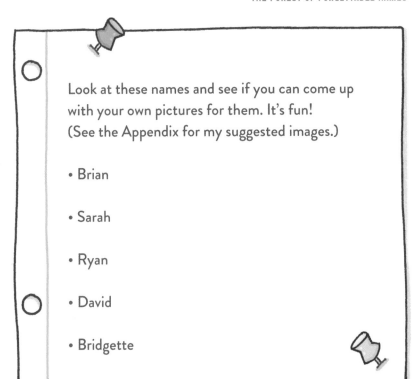

Look at these names and see if you can come up with your own pictures for them. It's fun!
(See the Appendix for my suggested images.)

• Brian

• Sarah

• Ryan

• David

• Bridgette

The next step is to **LINK**. Let's take that *name picture* and attach it to something we already know. In the case of names and faces, the best thing to attach the image to is the person's face since we're typically looking at it when we meet them. And usually, we notice things about their face. Maybe they have a nice smile or a goofy one. Perhaps they have freckles or just a small mole on their cheek. Everyone has something! And whenever we see that person again, we will always see the same thing. So why not use it as the thing we **LINK** our picture to?

Just always try to choose something on the person's face that jumps out at you *immediately*; something you know will jump out at you every time you see the person. Here are some common examples of things to look out for:

(Be very careful when doing this not to say the thing you noticed on the person's face, *out loud*. Sometimes the feature you notice might be a little bit embarrassing for them, so just keep the thought inside your head. This name-remembering technique is only for helping you get better at remembering names, not for making fun of anyone or making them feel bad. Nobody is perfect and we all have little things—whether good or bad—that people might notice.)

The last step is to **GO!** That means taking your image and attaching it to that person's face and sprinkling it with some imaginative spice! Ask yourself why the image is there. What is it doing? Use your senses. Make it move. Make it gross. Is it funny? Add as many memorable details as you can!

We've almost made it to the top of the tree and you've now got the idea of how memorizing names is done, so let's try it with Wickley's name for some extra practice before we reach the king. I'll help you with this one.

When I try to **SEE** the name Wickley, I can't really think of anything straight away—it's a pretty strange one. Unfortunately, I don't have any friends or family members named Wickley either. Hmm, does it sound like anything familiar? Sure. It kind of sounds like a mix between *wick* and *wiggly*? There you have it! My image for the name Wickley, will be a *wiggly* candle*wick—wick-ley*.

Next, let's **LINK**: Choose something on Wickley's face. How about his big red scraggly beard? That's perfect!

Finally, let's **GO!** I'm going to imagine that *wiggly* candle*wick* wiggling all up in his beard. So much so, that it causes the candle*wick* to catch fire, which then makes the beard catch fire as well, bursting into a big red ball of flame (and that's why his beard is red!). To make that image even more memorable, let's use all of our senses. Let's make sure to imagine the sound of a candlewick wiggling inside a scraggly beard. That makes me imagine a really scratchy sound. How about what it would feel like? Or what the burning beard hair would smell like. Is our image making us laugh out loud? Yep, it is for me! Is it gross? Check. Is there movement? Double check. Looks like we've got this picture **GO!**-ing already!

One last extra tip for remembering names. When you're done with the **SEE-LINK-GO!** process, ALWAYS use the person's name in a sentence *out loud* and as soon as possible. The sooner you do this, the better. Doing this helps because it allows your brain a chance to review what just happened, and reviewing things makes things stick for much longer. Here are a few different ways you can sneakily use the person's name out loud:

○ **Ask the person a question, but start or end the question with their name.**

For example: "Wickley, how much longer till we reach the top?"

○ **Maybe talk to a nearby person about the person's name you just learned.**

For example, you might say to me: "Hey, Nelson, you see Wickley over there? He's a pretty cool elf."

○ **Ask the person about their name. Make some conversation about it.**

For example: "Where is the name Wickley from? Did your father choose that name?"

Aha! Just in time! We've reached the top of the tree. Wickley pushes open a big wooden door and right before us appears a very regal elf with a huge nose sitting on a throne made of hundreds of branches. He looks sad and a bit bored . . . probably because he can't remember anything and because he's been stuck up on his throne for so long. Hopefully, we can help him out!

"Good day, almighty king of the Forgettable Names Forest! We have come here to help you remember your name and the names of people closest to you," I say to the king.

"Don't bother . . . I'm beyond help at this point," the king shamefully replies as he turns his head downward.

"I beg to differ, Your Majesty. Your kind guard over there, whose name is . . . uh . . . er . . ."

Psst . . . Quickly, what was the elf guard's name? I seem to have forgotten it!

Think of the feature we chose on his face, then see if you can remember the picture that comes to your mind. That should help you remember the name!

". . . WICKLEY. He was so kind as to guide us to you, and it seems like your people could do with a good lesson in memorizing names. Maybe if we shared our secret memory tricks, you'd all be able to remember each other's names. And your own!" I explain to the king.

He seems unconvinced, but eventually caves in and agrees to let us teach him the techniques. I spend the next few minutes explaining **SEE-LINK-GO!** and then ask him for the names of his mother, father, and brother (who are seated nearby watching).

"Let's start with your family members' names," I tell him. "If I can help you remember them with these techniques, maybe it will jog your memory for your own! Let's begin. Can you all take out your ID cards, please? Except for you, Your Majesty, I know you've lost yours—we'll get to your name in just a bit!"

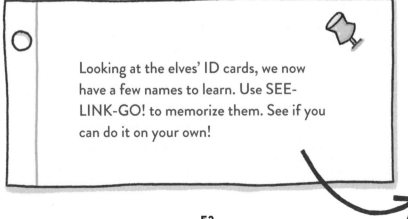

Looking at the elves' ID cards, we now have a few names to learn. Use SEE-LINK-GO! to memorize them. See if you can do it on your own!

In case you need a little inspiration, here's how I would have done it. Remember, this isn't the only way to do it, this is just the way I would have:

ELECTRA—Electric // She has long eyelashes, right? I would imagine her eyelashes being electric, shooting out electric sparks all over the place. Crazy, I know, but unforgettable.

CORNELL—Corn-L // Makes me think of an ear of corn, but it's bent into the shape of the letter L. Imagine, attached to his earlobes, are big yellow ears of corn, bent into Ls. Maybe he's even wearing them like earrings! I laughed out loud for that one! HA HA!

GROVER—Rover // Grover rhymes with rover. I think of a Mars rover (you know, those robot vehicles they send up into space to land on Mars?). When I think of the Mars rover, I think of this big metallic object slamming down on the surface of a planet and then driving around, exploring the place. Maybe instead of slamming it down on a planet, we slam it down on top of his cool surfer hairdo and have it investigate that instead! That's so weird!

After thinking about these names, we explain our mental pictures to the king. He closes his eyes for a second, thinking hard, then nods and suddenly cheers with joy. "I remember their names! Electra, Cornell, and Grover! It's been so long since I knew their names. But I still can't remember my own name . . ."

"Not to worry, Your Majesty. Do you happen to have a mirror?" I ask. "Let's see if you can notice your memorable feature and then remember your own name."

Wickley goes and fetches a large mirror and places it in front of the king. As the king takes a long look at himself, he suddenly lights up.

"Wait a minute . . . something's happening in my brain . . . I can feel it . . . I see my big nose, that's clearly my most noticeable feature . . . and now I'm starting to remember a picture of a wig hanging at the tip of my nose . . . Hmmm . . . The wig was flooding with water, yes! I remember now! A *flood-wig*. That *flood-wig* hanging at the end of my nose, seeping gallons of water . . . *FLOOD-WIG* . . . Ludwig! My name is Ludwig! I'll never be able to forget that now! Oh, thank you, thank you, thank you!"

"All hail King Ludwig!" everyone shouts in unison.

"Since we have helped you and your people, King Ludwig, would it be okay to ask something of *you*?" I ask.

"But of course, anything . . ."

"We are in search of a missing key piece. If we have the whole key, it will help us get to the Memory Thief—he's the one making us so forgetful these days. Last we heard, you had one of these pieces. I believe it is a treasure that you keep very safe."

Rubbing his chin with his hand, King Ludwig thinks to himself for a moment and gets up from his throne to walk over to a nearby wooden chest. He opens it, revealing a shiny fragment of metal with a pattern etched all over the surface.

A MISSING KEY PIECE!

"We elves are forever indebted to you," the king says, handing it to us. "We would be happy for you to take this treasure. I hope it helps you on your endeavor!"

We thank the king and his family (and Wickley, too) and tell him that we must be on our way. We say goodbye and wind our way back down to the forest floor.

Where to now? you must be thinking.

To be completely honest, I'm not sure. I only knew where the first key piece was. I was hoping we'd learn some information along the way about the second portion. But nope . . . nothing.

"Guys! Hold up!"

We turn to see Wickley, huffing and puffing.

"King Ludwig had something more to tell you. He's just getting the hang of this memory thing, so it only came to him after you had already left. He said something about the second piece of the key . . . that if you want to find it, you'll have to head to the end of the forest. There, you'll discover a vast and dangerous desert. If you travel far enough, and long enough, just until you think you can't go any farther, when it's too hot and you're too tired to go on, you'll reach the Great Word Pyramids. King Ludwig said they hold another piece of the key."

We look at each other and fist-bump.

"Thank you, Wickley!" we shout to him as we run off in the direction of the desert.

It seems that from here on out, our journey is only going to get tougher. You did great back there, remembering those names. I'm proud of you. You've got a real knack for this memory stuff. But I've still got so much to teach you and there are some new skills you'll need to have before we get to the pyramids. Shall we proceed?

And with that, we head down the forest path into the distance and toward the looming dangers of the Great Word Pyramids!

Here are a few more pictures of people you can practice memorizing names with. Once you think you have them memorized, cover the names and test yourself! (See the Appendix for my suggested images.)

Trish

William

Mary

CHAPTER 4

The Great Word Pyramids

HOW TO REMEMBER SPELLING, DEFINITIONS, AND FOREIGN LANGUAGES

Three long, hot, and sweaty days.

That's how long it's been since we left the forest and entered the desert. It seems to be never-ending, with not even a single pyramid in sight. Only rolling sand dune after sand dune, with the scorching sun overhead, melting us slowly. We climb up one dune only to see dozens more in front of us in the distance.

Could King Ludwig have been mistaken? Or could he have forgotten the correct directions and given us the wrong ones? Or even worse, could he be working with the Memory Thief and have set us on the wrong path on purpose? Although, he *did* say that we would have to keep going until we couldn't anymore, and that *only* then would we reach the pyramids. But what does that mean exactly? How much longer? We're running out of food, water, patience, and most important, brain power.

Over the past few days, we've reviewed everything that's happened to us and all the things you've learned so far. I've tried to prepare you for what's about to come. But to be completely honest, I'm not entirely sure what's next. See, I've heard about the Great Word Pyramids, but not much. And the little that I do know, I seem to have forgotten most of it . . .

Uh-oh . . . Do you think the Memory Thief is slowly stealing my memory already?

There is one small fact I forgot to mention about the Memory Thief. It turns out that he is stealing people's memories in order from oldest to youngest. I'm not horribly old, but I am older than you. The fact that my memory seems to be getting worse day by day is troubling. Remember when I couldn't remember the elf guard's name in the previous chapter? Ah, I actually can't quite think of it now, either . . . What was it again? Do you remember?

And these pyramids . . . I'm having such a hard time remembering everything I had heard about them. There was something about a crypt and a pharaoh . . . and something about some word tests . . . Ah yes, to get to the pharaoh's crypt in the center of the main pyramid, there are a few memory tests that we have to navigate in order to continue. But what were the tests? Hmmm . . . I can't seem to remember any more than that. And where would the key piece be? Hopefully, the pharaoh knows . . .

The fact that my memory is now fading pretty quickly means that time is running out. Before the end of our journey, I might not even be able to remember anything. And you'll be next! Once my memory is gone, you'll be the only person who can save all of our memories!

Let's pick up the pace. We've got to keep going and find those pyramids. Until we get there, I can try to give you as many memory tips as possible. That way, we'll be prepared for any kind of tests that lie ahead! Sound good?

Let's jump right in.

We've already memorized words like names of people and presidents, but what about remembering noun-y kinds of words, their spellings or vocabulary meanings? Or what about words in a different language and what they mean? Or even countries or states and their capitals?

Here are some examples of what I mean:

☑ **SPELLING** Example: Lieutenant—
L-i-e-u-t-e-n-a-n-t

☑ **VOCABULARY** Example: Evident—
plain or obvious; clearly seen or understood

☑ **FOREIGN WORDS** Example: *Baleine*—
a whale (in French)

☑ **COUNTRIES AND CAPITALS**
Example: Afghanistan—Kabul or Georgia—Atlanta

☑ **FLAGS** Example: Tanzania

We'll need to have a clever strategy to attack memorizing them all so that we can get to the center of this crypt. And hopefully, just *hopefully*, we'll find the second key piece there. You can even use what you learn on this part of our journey to memorize general facts that you need to know for school.

In the same way that we used **SEE-LINK-GO!** in the previous chapters, we can also follow the same steps to help us memorize these kinds of word-related things.

The basic idea is simple (and we've already kind of been doing it already, so it shouldn't be too hard for you): Take the word you're looking at and come up with a mental picture for it. Then, take the other word, spelling rule, definition, or whatever it is that the original word represents and come up with a picture for that, too. Then link them together in a fun and memorable way. I've basically just explained **SEE-LINK-GO!** again, haven't I?

Spelling

Let's start with remembering how to spell words. I bet you're already a great speller, but like all of us, there are usually a few words that give us problems and that we *always* forget how to spell. Was the *e* before the *i*? Is it a *ch* or a *sch*? Was it two *m*'s or just one? Sound familiar?

Learning the spelling of something is fun because you **LINK** the word you're trying to remember how to spell to some funny rule that *involves* the word somehow. It's like combining the **SEE-LINK-GO!** process all in one go.

Here are some examples of common words people misspell and a way to **SEE-LINK-GO!** a word all together so you never forget each one! Try this on any other spelling words that give you problems!

BELIEVE

● **BELIEVE** Never **belie*ve** a lie.

This is a great one because it's so obvious! Never believe a lie . . . Of course, why would I ever believe a lie?! This will help you remember that the word *lie* sits right in the middle of *believe*.

● **LIEUTENANT** "Lie, u ten ants!" the lieutenant yelled at the ten ants.

How silly is that? Picture a mean lieutenant all dressed up in uniform yelling at ten tiny little ants to not tell the truth.

LIE! YOU TEN ANTS!

● **SEPARATE**
There's *a rat* in **sepa*rat*e**.

Imagine a stinky, icky rat sneaking right in the middle of that word, trying to separate it. There literally is "a rat" in the middle of *separate*.

● **DESSERT** This one is easy. The extra s is because you always want extra *dessert*!

This can help you remember the difference between *dessert* and *desert*. A *desert* is big, vast, and empty . . . almost like it's missing something . . . an *s*! *Desert* is missing that extra *s*, while *dessert* has it!

● **CARIBBEAN** Imagine there are two *big boats* sailing in the middle of that word. CariBBean! That will help you to remember those double *b*'s.

Vocabulary Meanings

How does one go about memorizing vocabulary words? Like I said before, it's a lot like remembering names. We see a word and its meaning (like a face and a name), so we come up with an image for both and then we **LINK** them together. You remember that process, right? With vocabulary words, it's a bit easier because we don't need a face to stick it to. Imagine that learning a new vocab word is like a math equation. The left-hand side (LHS) of the equation is the word we're trying to memorize, while the right-hand side (RHS) of the equation is the short (or long) definition. Coming up with an image for the left-hand word is something we know how to do very well, it's just **SEE**. But the right-hand side is tougher because it's usually going to be a few words together in a sentence. How on earth do we memorize *that*?

It's not too hard, actually. Just read the definition and think of a picture that captures the main idea. It doesn't have to be word for word. That's too hard. Keep it simple and focus on what it says and keep it as short as possible. Once you have that image, link it to the image you had for the left-side word. And of course, don't forget to **GO!** Make that image super memorable! The next time you hear the word or you hear the definition, you'll be able to remember the opposite side of the equation. Here are some examples of words with all the memorization parts worked out for you already:

● EVIDENT—plain or obvious; clearly seen or understood.

First, we need an image for the word on the LHS. *Evident* sounds like *heavy dent*. So I might picture a car with a heavy dent in the hood (like something heavy has dropped on it and caused the dent). For the RHS, we've got a lot of words. Let's clean it up and try to give it a shorter definition.

Maybe just the word *obvious*? I think that word captures the definition pretty well. So now let's **LINK** it all together and **GO!** I'll imagine a car with a *heavy dent* and think: "Something heavy would make a dent, *obviously*. Everyone that passes the car says, 'Oh wow, that's a *heavy dent*! It's SO *obvious*!'" That's all we need for this one!

● FRIVOLOUS—not worthy of serious notice.

My image for *frivolous* could be *shrivel*, since I can't really think of anything else and *frivol*(ous) rhymes with *shrivel*(ous). The definition of the word is hard to picture, so instead, let's break it down a bit: When I think of a *serious notice*, I think of a serious note that says some kind of official government warning on it. It's a *serious notice*. If something isn't worthy, I imagine someone on their knees chanting, "We're *not worthy*, we're *not worthy*!" So let's imagine someone doing just that, on their knees chanting, "We're *not worthy*" at a *serious notice* on the wall. They do it so much that the note *shrivels* up! Voilà!

● BOISTEROUS—noisily jolly or rowdy.

Boisterous is a hard word, so I'll break it into syllables and see if that helps for **SEE**ing. Boi-ster-ous: *boy staring* (at) *us* (boy-stare-us) I'll picture a boy staring at us awkwardly. *Noisily jolly* I think of someone laughing really loud. Since it's jolly, maybe that reminds me of Santa! Ho, Ho, Ho!

He's always jolly and loud when he laughs, right? So our story is: Imagine seeing a *boy staring* at us and Santa *jolly* and laughing *noisily* back at him. See? This is fun!

Try this out on your own vocabulary words that you need to learn for school. Or try memorizing these definitions on your own. (See Appendix to see how I would do it.)

TRY THIS AT HOME!

- *Indignant*—expressing strong displeasure at something offensive.
- *Teem*—to abound or swarm; be prolific or fertile.
- *Protrude*—to thrust forward.

Foreign Words

What about foreign-language words? In my opinion, they're easier to memorize because the LHS (the foreign word) is almost meaningless to you when you first look at it. Since you have no idea of what that word might mean, you can make it as crazy as you want.

To memorize a word in another language, I typically come up with a picture for the word based on either how it's spelled (maybe it looks like an English word I know) or how it sounds (maybe it sounds like a funny version of an English word I know). Then I attach it to an image for what the word means (that's the RHS of the equation). The best way to understand is by example. Let's try a few fun ones in French, since I grew up speaking that language:

● *CHOU*—cabbage

Chou (pronounced identically to "shoe") is a funny little word I heard a lot as a kid because my parents would call each other that. Calling each other "cabbage" is kind of strange, I know, but in French it sounds sweet! Because the word sounds like "shoe" and means "cabbage," if we **LINK** the two sides of the equation, we can create a memorable image of a shoe stomping on a cabbage and destroying it. STOMP! STOMP! STOMP! Not so sweet, but memorable!

● *BALEINE*—whale

Something about this word just feels so light and fluffy to me. It's a beautiful word. *Baleine* (pronounced "bah-lenn") kinda-sorta sounds

like "balloon." (Remember, it doesn't need to be *exactly* the same, just something close enough to help us remember the original word.) **LINK**ing it with the definition of a whale, we can imagine a balloon being filled with air inside of a whale, causing it to grow and grow into the massive mammal it is! Maybe it even fills up with so much air that it floats up into the sky just like a balloon. Weird, but memorable.

● *PAMPLEMOUSSE*—grapefruit

This is a funny one. It (pronounced "pump-luh-moose") sounds like pumping a moose, so I would picture me pumping up a moose (using some kind of large tire pump) with grapefruits. Actual grapefruits are being pumped into the body of a moose. What?! Yup. It's as simple as that.

Now you try! See if you can learn a few of these funny French words. If you need some help, have a peek in the Appendix.

- *Cerf-volant* (pronounced surf-vol-aunt)—kite

- *Souris* (pronounced sue-ree)—mouse

- *Débile* (pronounced deh-beel)—silly, dumb

States and Capitals

To remember U.S. states and their capitals, it's no different than everything we've done so far in this chapter . . . Well, except that it's even easier, since the "definition" is just a single word—the capital—not an entire sentence. You could honestly learn all the state capitals in less than thirty minutes. We won't go through them all right now, but you can find the rest of them in one of my online videos.

● **Delaware—Dover**

Think of a *doll wearing* (doll-wear = Delaware) a *dove* (dove = Dover) as her clothes.

DOLL WEAR + DOVE

Pennsylvania—Harrisburg

Think of *Dracula* with *pens* as his fangs (Dracula is from Transylvania, but with pens in his mouth it's *Penn-sylvania*) taking a big juicy bite out of a *hairy-burger* (Harrisburg).

PENS-SYLVANIA
+
HAIRY BURGER

A NEW JERSEY
JAMES
+ TENTS ON

New Jersey—Trenton

Think as if you've just been given a brand-*new jersey* from your favorite athlete (maybe LeBron James?), and when you look at it really close-up you notice hundreds of little *tents on* it (tents-on = Trenton).

Georgia—Atlanta

Think of *George* of the Jungle swinging from vine to vine and a *bat landing* on his arm in mid-swing (bat-land = At-lant-a).

GEORGE +
BAT LANDING

CONNECT-CUT

HEART FORD

Connecticut—Hartford

This one's simple! Just think of *connecting* (Connect-i-cut) a bloody, beating *heart* to a *Ford* pickup truck (heart-Ford = Hartford)! Beep! Beep! And then *cutting* it in half (Connect-cut = Connecticut).

Countries and Capitals

Let's try the exact same thing but with some countries around the world. The only difference here is that some of these words might be a little stranger to you since you probably haven't heard or seen them as often as the United States. We'll only cover a few right now, but if you want to learn *all* 195 countries and their capitals, you can find them in another one of my online videos.

● Afghanistan—Kabul

An *Afghan* hound dog (you know, those tall, pointy-nosed, long-haired dogs?) driving a *cab* with a *bull* in the back seat (cab-bull = Kabul). If you've never seen an Afghan dog before, you can think of something else. How about *half-can-stand*? That almost sounds identical to Afghanistan. You can picture *half* of a *can stand*ing, which then drives a *cab* with a *bull* in the back seat. Either way, you'll never forget that capital, will you?

● Montenegro—Podgorica

A *mountain growing* (mountain-grow = Montenegro) out of a string bean *pod* and a Thanksgiving-style *gourd* (pod-gourd = Podgorica).

Estonia—Tallinn

Imagine a *stone* (Estonia) being thrown at a very *tall inn* (tall=inn).

Bahrain—Manama

Imagine balking at the rain, saying, "BAH! RAIN!" as you dance and sing that silly song from *The Muppet Show*: "Ma-na, ma-na, doo doo, do do do . . ."

Morocco—Rabat

You've got a pile of rocks. More and MORE *rocks* (more-rocks = Morocco) and you throw them all at some pesky *rabbits* that are ruining your backyard (rabbit = Rabat). Simple as that!

Flags and Maps

You can even do this process with words that have a picture or shape as their definition, like a flag. You have the name of a country and then a colorful, rectangular shape as its "definition." Or a country on a map— you have the name of a country and then the outline of a shape as its "definition."

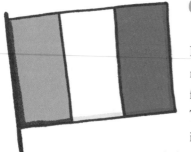

Italy

Notice that this flag goes green-white-red (from left to right). What is Italy's favorite and most commonly used food? Tomatoes, right?! (Since they use them in pizza and all those pasta sauces.) A tomato starts green and then eventually turns ripe to red! So, from left to right we have green, white, then red. Simple as that!

Canada

This is a pretty memorable flag already, centered around that red maple leaf. Imagine stuffing a bunch of maple leaves in a *can of dye*, making the leaf all red (*can-of-dye* = Canada).

Tanzania

This is a tough one. Notice the flag is green on the upper left triangular half and blue on the lower right. Right in the middle is a black line bordered by two thinner yellow lines. Now imagine that the green is grass and the blue is the ocean. The diagonal strip in the middle is a beach, which if you lie on it for a long time, you'll end up with a *tan* that's *zany*! A black-and-yellow-striped tan! So zany! (*Tan-zany* = Tanzania.)

74

● France

To remember the shape of France on a map, look at the shape of the country and see what it reminds you of. To me, I see a Frenchman with his arms outstretched, eating a long baguette sandwich.

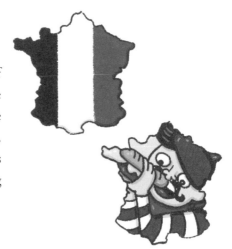

● Cameroon

The outline of Cameroon looks like a rooster perched up, looking to his right. The name of the country makes me think of a combination of *camera* and *maroon* (which is a dark red color). So, imagine taking a picture with your *camera* of a *maroon rooster*!

Isn't it so simple? I could teach you these all day! But we have to get on with our journey. Let's try something that's a little more difficult and then we'll start thinking about where to find shelter for the night. It's getting late and the sun is setting soon. I just hope we can find those pyramids . . .

Facts

Now let's talk about memorizing facts. Facts are a bit trickier since they're not necessarily a single word on one side or the other. Learning how to memorize things like this are helpful for a lot of the facts you need to remember in school. This can also aid you if you ever have a multiple-choice test and need to read a question and remember the answer that goes along with it.

The technique works the same as before. Think of a picture for one side, think of another picture for the other side, link them together and make it memorable. Let's try a few:

● **The three branches of the U.S. government— Executive, Legislative, and Judicial**

The LHS is long and hard to remember word for word. But let's just imagine the Capitol building with three big branches growing out of it. This will help us remember *government* and *three branches*. On the RHS we have three big, difficult words. Hmmm . . . Let's add some detail to each branch to help us remember these three complicated words!

Executive—kind of sounds like *ax-cut*. It's not the whole word, but it's enough to remind me of *executive*. So, imagine an ax cutting down that first branch.

Legislative—makes me think of *legs* and *late-night TV* (legs-late-TV). Imagine seeing a lot of legs on late-night TV. Ooh la la! Let's mentally stick that TV to the second branch.

Judicial—sounds like someone shouting, *"Chew the*

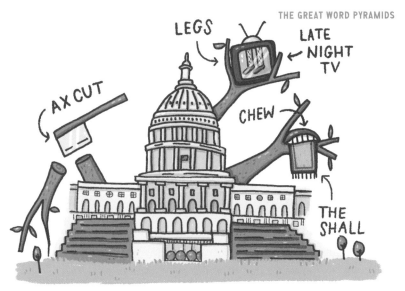

shawl!" Imagine someone yelling that at the third branch and you see it actually chewing on a shawl. Ha ha!

The five Great Lakes—Huron, Ontario, Michigan, Erie, Superior

Sometimes, we have an answer that contains a lot of information . . . Those five lake names are a lot to remember. We can use a special technique called *chunking* to group everything together. To do this, we can create an acronym. Let's use the word HOMES. Think of a big lake suddenly opening up in the floor of your HOMES (I know you probably only have one home, but for this example to work, let's imagine you have many HOMES). H is for Huron, O is for Ontario, and so on. If you have trouble remembering the names of the lakes themselves, you can always add extra details to your picture to help jog your memory. Maybe inside your HOMES there is a lot of *hair on* the furniture (hair-on = Huron). Or maybe think of your HOMES as being *superior* to all of your friends' homes (that's Lake Superior). You get the picture!

Okay, I think by now you've gotten the idea of how this works. You're well practiced at this point and I am getting pretty tired. Aren't you? We've walked for almost four days straight in the desert (not dessert, right? Although I could do with a dessert right about now!) and there looks to be no end in sight.

Eventually, we come across a very tall dune. One so tall that it blocks the sun and finally gives us a nice bit of shade to hide behind. We rest a bit, but then look at each other and nod—we must march on. It's getting late and we need to find those pyramids before it gets dark, even if it means climbing up this enormous sand dune. Hopefully from the top we'll be able to see the pyramids. So up we go.

After an hour of slogging along, one foot after the other, we're both just a few steps away from the very top.

One more step and . . . we've made it. I slowly look up, hoping to see some form of pyramid in the distance and . . .

NOPE. Nothing. Just a whole lot more desert, as far as the eye can see.

You tap me on the shoulder and spin me around.

"OH! Whoops! There they are! I was looking in the wrong direction. I must be really tired," I say aloud.

Right below us, at the base of the dune, stand three large pyramids with hundreds of words scribbled all over them. The Great Word Pyramids! We've finally arrived! One of the three pyramids (the largest one in the center) has a large opening.

That must be the way in! Let's head for it.

We're running so fast, we practically slide down the sandy slope and arrive at the entrance. As we step inside, we grab a nearby lit torch to help us find our way through the dark and eerie corridor. It's not too long before we run into a stone wall with some engravings on it. Aha, some instructions!

Welcome adventurer, you have reached the first word test of the Great Word Pyramids. Do you dare continue? The task is simple . . . or so it may seem. I will give you five country names paired with their capitals. Learn the pairings. And then continue through the door. There, you will find some ancient clay tiles, each with the words etched on them. You'll need to arrange the tiles in pairs—the correct country with its correct capital. Once you do that, a mummy will come out of his tomb and make sure they are correct. If they are, the mummy will open the gate to the next room. But fail and you will remain here forever!

Here are the countries and capitals:

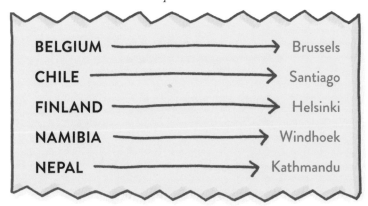

Such difficult words! But we can do it. Just remember how I taught you to memorize the country or state capitals from before. Come up with a picture and **SEE** it for the LHS, then the RHS, then **LINK** and **GO!** You know the deal!

My memory isn't doing too well at the moment . . . Not sure if it's me just being tired or if the Memory Thief is really getting to me, but you're on your own with this task. Just remember what I taught you and I'll be here to support you.

Take out a sheet of paper and write down the five countries from page 79. Memorize the capitals, and when you feel ready, close this book and see if you can remember them!). Don't advance until you get it right without peeking! (Check the Appendix for some suggestions).

We walk into the next room and you start arranging the tiles in the correct pairs. As soon as you finish placing the last piece in its correct order, we hear a slow shuffling behind us. Turning around, we see a mummy, arms outstretched, groaning softly. The mummy spends a minute looking over the arranged tiles, making all sorts of strange mummy-murmuring sounds as he confirms your answers.

"MmmahmmmmMMM!" the mummy says, nodding his head and pointing to a now visible gate, creaking open, way in the back corner of the room.

Nice job, kiddo! You're a pro at this memory stuff! It looks like he's telling us to continue on to the next and final challenge. Let's do this!

Into the final room we go, and again we're met with a stone wall with some engravings on them:

Well done, adventurer! But the first test was easy. Now for the final test. You must answer the following questions I will randomly ask you. One mistake, and you will . . . remain here forever! If you accept the challenge, step forward.

We step forward.

A booming voice shakes the room. "WHAT IS THE CAPITAL OF PENNSYLVANIA?" it asks.

You know this one! Think back to earlier in our journey, what image did we come up with for Pennsylvania? What was the capital of that state?

You say the answer.

"CORRECT. TAKE ANOTHER STEP!"

We step forward again.

"QUESTION TWO: WHAT DOES THE WORD BOISTEROUS MEAN?"

What are the chances! We know this one, too! Can you remember the definition of *boisterous*?

You say the answer.

"VERY GOOD. ONE LAST STEP!"

We take one more step forward.

"LAST QUESTION: HOW DO YOU SAY 'KITE' IN FRENCH?"

Oh, that's a tough one, but it's one of the questions I gave you in an exercise. Did you do it? I hope so, otherwise we're in trouble . . .

Again, you say the answer.

Nothing happens for a moment . . .

Did we get it correct? What's going to happen next?

Out of the silence we suddenly hear a "Congratulations!" from behind us. We turn around and see an ancient pharaoh clapping slowly, clearly very impressed with the two of us for having made it all the way through to the center of the pyramid.

"Well done to the both of you for making it through those difficult word tests. I have been trapped in here for thousands of years, held here against my will by an awful curse, and you have finally freed me. The curse could only be broken if someone made it through all the challenges. You two are the only ones who have ever done that! Thank you!" the pharaoh explains.

"Also, it is only fair that I reward you for the freedom you have given me. Tell me what you would like and it will be yours!"

We look at each other and yell, "THE PIECE OF THE KEY TO THE GATES OF MOUNT FOREVEREST!"

"Somehow I knew you would ask for that. Apparently, it leads to some kind of treasure if you have the other pieces . . . or so I've heard . . ."

We look at each other, confused. Treasure? All we know is that it leads to the Memory Thief. Could there be more to this key than we know? We can worry about that later. For now, though, let's get the second piece and get out of here. Time is running out!

The pharaoh reaches into a fold in his linen tunic and pulls out the key fragment to hand to us when . . .

"ARGHHHHHH!!!!!" we hear a few unknown voices shout around the room.

BOOM! CLANG! BOOM! CLANG!

Suddenly, everything goes dark.

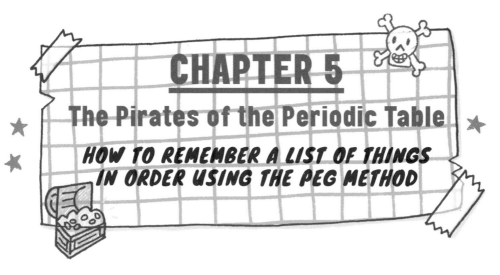

CHAPTER 5
The Pirates of the Periodic Table
HOW TO REMEMBER A LIST OF THINGS IN ORDER USING THE PEG METHOD

BOOMs and CLANGs were the last sounds we heard before everything went dark. Somehow we were knocked out and now find ourselves in a dim-lit, wet, and stinky prison. From the way it smells (salty and fishy) and moves (the floor under us is rolling slowly up and down), I'd guess that we're actually in the belly of a big ship sailing on the ocean.

How on earth did we get here from the desert? Those noises we heard in the pyramids . . . what were they? And why is my head so sore?

I rub my fingers through my hair and feel a small bump. I must have been hit over the head with something and then taken prisoner aboard someone's ship! And you, too, by the looks of it. But why? And by whom?

Uh-oh. The key piece.

Do you remember what happened to it? I ask you.

You shake your head . . .

I vaguely recall that you helped us pass the word tests in the pyramid, that we met a pharaoh in the crypt, that he was about to give us the key piece, and that there were some loud sounds . . . a loud screaming of "ARGHHHH!" before everything went dark. Hopefully we'll get some answers soon. For now, we need to find a way out of here.

Looking around, we notice something very odd. Not only are we in separate prison cells, near to each other, but there are dozens of jail cells around us containing all sorts of different animals. I seem to be the only elephant and you the only human, and all the others are different. In the cells next to me are a dog on one side and a frog on the other. For you, a big iguana and a giraffe. How strange, indeed!

Suddenly, up above we hear a lock being rattled and then opened.

KASHLINK! The roof hatch flies open and a funny-looking pirate with a wooden peg leg plops down in front of our cell.

"ARGHHH! Ye mateys! Ye be my prisoners!" he snarls at us.

I knew it! We've been kidnapped by some pirates. They must have followed behind us as we passed all the word tests in the pyramid. Perhaps they're after the key pieces as well. The pharaoh had mentioned something about treasure. Maybe that's what they're after. But why are they keeping us prisoner? Why not take the key piece and leave? I don't like the look of this!

"Argh! Thank ye for leadin' us to the secret key piece in the pyramid! We are lookin' for the other pieces so we can get to the treasure.

Do ye know about the other ones? Argh. We are on our way to get the third piece, but not sure where the first is . . ."

We shake our heads. Thankfully, they don't seem to know about the first fragment we already have. Better not let them find out!

"Where are we headed?" I ask.

"To the Himalayan **MEMORY PALACE**, of course! Argh! It's the gateway to Mount Foreverest, after all, where at the top we shall find all the treasure in the world! Argh!" the pirate explains while tapping his pipe on his peg leg. "My name is Peg the Pirate, as ye can see from my peg leg here. And I am part of the pirate crew called the Pirates of the Periodic Table. We sure do love the periodic table! Yes, we do. ARGH!"

Treasure? At the top of Mount Foreverest? He must be mistaken . . . or maybe the Memory Thief has gotten to him already and he's forgotten what's *really* up there.

"Why did you imprison us?" I ask.

"Ye both seem smart, argh! Who knows what kind of smartness I'll need on the mountain to claim my treasure! Also, you complete my collection of beasts. As ye may have noticed, I have an animal here for every letter of the alphabet. Ye mateys are the letter *E* for *Elephant* and *H* for *Human*! ARGH!"

And with that, he manages to leap back up through the hatch, slamming the door behind him.

We look around and realize that there is indeed one animal for every letter of the alphabet, each in their own cell, and alphabetically ordered. How curious!

Let's try to memorize all these animals quickly, just in case. You never know—maybe it'll come in handy later on when we try to escape . . .

Since the animals are in the order of the alphabet, it shouldn't even really feel like memorizing. You know the alphabet already, right? You know it so well you don't even need to think about it if you want to say it. So adding an animal that matches each letter should be a breeze.

Looking around the big prison, here are the animals we see:

NOTE TO READER

Again, don't try to memorize these with a technique. The fact that they are alphabetized will make this very easy. Most of the animals you'll see are ones you'd probably think of anyway. Like, hey, think of an animal that starts with a *t*. I bet you thought of a tiger, didn't you? See what I mean? The obvious animal is typically the correct one on this ship.

A = Alligator

B = Bear

C = Cat

D = Dog

E = Elephant (me)

F = Frog

G = Giraffe

H = Human (you)

I = Iguana

J = Jellyfish

K = Kangaroo

L = Lion

M = Monkey

N = Newt (that's a small lizard)

O = Owl

P = Panda

Q = Quail (a small bird)

R = Rhino

S = Snake

T = Tiger

U = Unicorn

V = Vulture

W = Whale

X = Xmas reindeer

Y = Yak

Z = Zebra

Now that you have that list in your head, we have to find a way out of here. While we're at it, we should also find a way to free these animals.

"Oh, look!" I point to a set of keys on the floor. "Peg the Pirate must have dropped them when he came into visit us. Those *have* to be the keys to our prison cells. If we can only reach them . . ."

You point to the giraffe in the cell next to you, who oddly has a pair of nitro boosters attached to his sides.

"I see where your head is at! Great idea!" I shout. Then, turning to the giraffe, I say, "Hey, giraffe! Can you shoot your nitro boosters at those keys and see if you can knock them toward either one of us?"

The giraffe nods and does exactly that. *BWOOOOOSHHHH!* The nitro boosters zip right between the prison bars, hitting the keys as they fly past, causing the keys to bounce over to a spot where I can reach them with my long elephant trunk.

"Nice!"

We open our cells and, starting with A, we open each of the other cells. But we suddenly realize that these are not normal animals . . . Each one of them has a very strange feature about them. What is going on here? Maybe it's important, so we better pay attention. As we make our way around the prison, freeing the animals, we notice the following weird scenarios:

- An **alligator** with a fire *hydrant* on its back

- A **bear** holding a *helium* balloon

- A **cat** with *lithium* batteries instead of paws

● A **dog** with a *barrel* for a torso

● An **elephant** (me) acting *bored* (I'm getting really bored in this cell, making really silly sounds and running around in circles. FIVE circles to be exact. What on earth?)

● A **frog** driving a *car*

● A **giraffe** with two *nitro* boosters strapped to his sides

● A **human** (you) Well, there's nothing too special about you other than you're breathing in *oxygen*.

● An **iguana** with a *flower* growing out of his forehead

● A **jellyfish** all lit up like a bright pink *neon* sign. Also, this jellyfish has exactly TEN tentacles (TENtacles!).

● A **kangaroo** drinking a *soda*

● A **lion** in the shape of a large *magnet*

● A **monkey** made of *aluminum* foil

● A **newt** covered in *silicon* computer chips

● FIFTEEN **owls** with *faucets* for wings
(For whatever reason, there were fifteen
owls in this cell, not sure why!)

● A **panda** sitting on a *sofa*

● A **quail** swimming in
a *chlorine*-filled pool

● A **rhino** *arguing* really
loudly with itself

● A **snake** slithering in
and out of a large *pot*

● A **tiger** chugging TWENTY
big glasses of *milk*

● A **unicorn** *scanning* some papers

● A **vulture** made of *titanium*
metal and as large as a *titan*

● A **whale** driving a *van*

● A **Xmas reindeer** on the internet using
a *chrome* bumper to pick his teeth

- A **yak** with TWENTY-FIVE *mangoes* all over him

- A **zebra** pumping *iron*

Pause for a moment and go through the alphabet and see if you can remember each strange image. You should be able to do it! If you miss one or two, no problem, just peek back at our list and relearn it. Then try again!

Just as we finish observing all the weirdness of the animals, the hatch flies open and a whole gang of pirates flood in.

"WHAT DO YE THINK YE ARE DOING? ARGH??" they shout.

We freeze. Uh-oh, we're in big trouble.

"SEIZE THEM!" Peg the Pirate orders.

They grab us and carry us up to the deck of the boat, then tie our legs and hands together.

"Ye must walk the plank, mateys!" Peg proclaims. "But we'll give ye one chance to win your freedom! We love the periodic table A LOT—even more than parrots and rum—so if you can answer some questions about it, we'll let you go! ARGH!!"

"First question: What is the first element on the periodic table?" Peg says with an evil smile, probably thinking we don't know anything about the subject.

Okay, kiddo. Do you know anything about the periodic table? Probably not, eh? I used to, but my memory is so bad now I can't remember *anything*.

Peg takes out his sword and points it at us, forcing us a little farther out onto the plank. A shark snout peeks out above the waves below and sniffs a little.

"Wait, something's just occurred to me!" I whisper to you. "The animals downstairs . . . they were all really bizarre, right? We couldn't figure out why, but I think I can now! Maybe each animal had something to do with an element on the periodic table. And since the alphabet is in order, maybe the first animal is linked to the first element, and so on."

Think back to your list of animals. Can you remember the one that went with the letter A? What was the silly image we had? What was on the animal's back? If you can remember it, then you should be able to make a clever guess as to what is the first element! See if you can figure it out. (Peek to the full list on page 96 if you can't!)

You shout out the answer to Peg the Pirate. His mouth drops. He can't believe you knew the answer.

"That . . . is . . . uh . . . correct . . . ARGH!! Another question!" He nudges us farther onto the plank. "What is the seventh element in the periodic table?"

You shout out the answer. He can't believe his ears!

"That . . . is . . . uh . . . also correct . . . ARGH!! ARGH!! One more question . . . You'll never get this one!" He nudges us even farther until we are at the very edge of the plank, nearly falling off. "What number element is chromium?"

What is the seventh animal? First think of the seventh letter of the alphabet, then think of which animal starts with that letter, then think of the weird image linked to that animal. Can you guess what element that is? (Peek to the chart again if you can't!)

You'll have to work backward for this one. First, scan your memory and see if you remember any of the animals having to do with chromium or something related to chrome. Do you remember any? Once you have an animal in your mind, you'll have to find out what number that letter is in the alphabet. You can either count from 1, if it's early in the alphabet, or count backward from 26, if it's later in the alphabet. Can you figure it out?

After thinking a moment, you say your answer.

"Correct again! ARGH!!! Boy am I disappointed I don't get to make you a meal for the sharks, but also incredibly impressed! And anyone who knows about the periodic table as much as I do should be a friend of mine, not an enemy! Ye mateys are free to go!" Peg declares as his pirate buddies rescue us from the plank and undo our bindings.

"Thank you for letting us go, Peg! But may we continue on with our adventure? We're both heading for the same mountain, but you should know you'll find no treasure there. Only an evil monster who is stealing everyone's memories. He's even stolen yours, which is probably why you thought there was treasure up on the mountain in the first place," I explain as I pull out the first key piece. "Look, we've secretly had this first key piece all along. Please give us your piece and take us to the Himalayan **MEMORY PALACE** so we can get the final fragment and complete the key. Please help us save everyone from losing their memories!"

"No wonder my memory has been so bad lately, ARGH! I will help the both of you. I want me memory back so I can find where the treasure really is! Argh! The key piece is in that treasure chest over there," Peg replies, pointing to an old wooden chest on the other side of the ship.

We head over and flip it open. It's empty except for one shiny metallic fragment that is the second part of the key. I connect the two together. They fit perfectly.

All we need is the last one! And thanks to the Pirates of the Periodic Table, we now know the last one is in the Himalayan **MEMORY PALACE**. Which is where we're headed. Great!

Nice job back there, buddy. I'm not sure if you were aware of it, but you used a new memory technique. One that I was going to teach you next. It's pretty funny that it was Peg the Pirate who taught it to you without him even knowing. The method is called **THE PEG METHOD**.

THE PEG METHOD is another memory technique that allows you to keep the order of a list of things you want to memorize. It's a very powerful way to do the **LINK** step of **SEE-LINK-GO!** And when a technique is *powerful*, that means it's *extra* sticky! Exactly what you want when memorizing long lists of things like the Periodic Table.

When you use this method, you'll know your lists forward and backward. You can even jump straight to different parts of the list. So you can tell what the thirteenth item is, or the twenty-fifth—any of them! You can do that because you've **LINK**ed your image to a peg. (*Peg* is a fancy word for "thing you already know.") So, just like you knew the alphabet already, we were able to **LINK** an image to each animal peg to help us remember the first twenty-six elements of the periodic table. Cool, right?

NOTE TO READER

Now, remember that some of your animal peg images had numbers as part of their image? For example, the jellyfish had TEN tentacles. If you were paying attention, you might have noticed the numbers went 5-10-15-20-25. The reason we included pictures of those numbers was to help us jump around the list if we wanted to. Say we wanted to recall the thirteenth element. Instead of counting from A up to the thirteenth letter of the alphabet, we could jump to fifteen. Remember the fifteen owls with faucets for wings? That was the fifteenth element. So the thirteenth letter would be two letters before O, which would be M = a monkey made of aluminum foil. The thirteenth element is aluminum!

In case you were curious what the other elements were, let's reveal them:

A · An Alligator with a fire *hydrant* on its back
Hydrant = **HYDROGEN**

B · A bear holding a *helium* balloon
Helium = **HELIUM**

C · A cat with *lithium* batteries instead of paws
Lithium = **LITHIUM**

D · A dog with a *barrel* for a torso
  Barrel = barrel-ium = **BERYLLIUM**

E · An elephant (me) acting *bored*, making silly
  sounds and running around in FIVE circles.
  Bored = **BORON**

F · A frog driving a *car*
  Car = **CARBON**

G · A giraffe with two *nitro* boosters
  strapped to his sides
  Nitro = **NITROGEN**

(YOU!)

H · A human (you) . . . Well, there's nothing
  too special about you other than you're
  breathing in *oxygen*.
  Oxygen = **OXYGEN**

I · An iguana with a *flower* growing
  out of his forehead
  Flower = **FLUORINE**

J · A jellyfish all lit up like a bright pink *neon*
  sign with TEN tentacles (TENtacles!)
  Neon = **NEON**

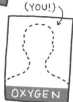

K · A kangaroo drinking a *soda*
  Soda = **SODIUM**

L · A lion in the shape of a large *magnet*
Magnet = **MAGNESIUM**

M · A monkey made of *aluminum* foil
Aluminum = **ALUMINUM**

N · A newt covered in *silicon*
computer chips
Silicon = **SILICON**

O · FIFTEEN owls with *faucets* for wings
Faucets = Fauce-phorous = **PHOSPHOROUS**

P · A panda sitting on a *sofa*
Sofa = **SULFUR**

Q · A quail swimming in
a *chlorine*-filled pool
Chlorine = **CHLORINE**

R · A rhino *arguing* really loudly with itself
Argue =**ARGON**

S · A snake slithering in and out of a large *pot*
Pot = **POTASSIUM**

T · A tiger chugging TWENTY big glasses of *milk*
Milk = **CALCIUM**
(since milk is filled with calcium)

U · A unicorn *scanning* some papers
Scanning = **SCANDIUM**

V · A vulture made of *titanium* metal
and as large as a *titan*
Titanium = **TITANIUM**

W · A whale driving a *van*
Van = **VANADIUM**

X · A Xmas reindeer using a *chrome*
bumper to pick his teeth
Chrome bumper = **CHROMIUM**

Y · A yak with TWENTY-FIVE
mangoes all over him
Mangoes = **MANGANESE**

Z · A zebra pumping *iron*
Iron weight = **IRON**

For a great exercise, see if you can name all twenty-
six elements in order from one to twenty-six. For an
added challenge, see if you can do it backward as well!
If you'd like to learn the rest (there are over a hundred
elements), check out the video on my website.

THE PERIODIC TABLE

1 HYDROGEN

3 LITHIUM

4 BERYLLIUM

5 BORON

6 CARBON

11 SODIUM

12 MAGNESIUM

13 ALUMINIUM

14 SILICON

19 POTASSIUM

20 CALCIUM

21 SCANDIUM

22 TITANIUM

KEY:

- ALKALI METALS
- NOBLE GASES
- ALKALINE-EARTH METALS
- TRANSITION METALS
- BASIC METALS
- HALOGEN GASES
- SEMI-METALS
- NON-METALS

I know what you're thinking . . . Is the alphabetic animal list the *only* peg list you can use for this method to work? NOPE! And that's the beauty of it. A peg list can be *any* list you already know. It has to be a list, though. The alphabet is an easy one, and you can also choose other categories as well—it doesn't always have to be animals. You could do foods, sports-related things, nouns, verbs, whatever! Instead of letters, you could also use numbers. You can count from one, onward, can't you? Well, if you have an image for each number, you can use them as pegs and attach images for things on those numbers.

NOTE TO READER

You may be wondering how to use these lists if you need to memorize different things often. Can you use the same list over and over again? Or should you create a new one each time? Think of the number of pegs you have as how much hard drive space you have on your mental computer. The more you have, the more you can store. But there are different kinds of things you might want to store in your brain. Maybe it's something you only need for a few hours and then you can forget it. Or maybe it's something you want to keep for the rest of your life. If it's for something you want to keep for a short time, then you can reuse a peg list. If it's something you want for longer, create a new one and only use it for that one thing you're trying to memorize. That way it always stays fresh.

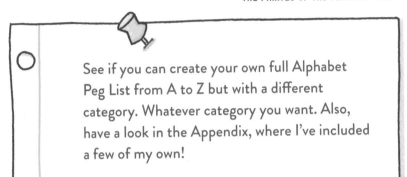

See if you can create your own full Alphabet Peg List from A to Z but with a different category. Whatever category you want. Also, have a look in the Appendix, where I've included a few of my own!

After a few days of sailing, taking care of all the animals on board, and getting to know our new pirate friends, mountains start to appear on the horizon—massive, towering peaks! And there in the very center of them all, one in particular looming over the rest . . . Mount Foreverest.

Peg the Pirate walks over to us and starts explaining what we should expect on the next leg of our journey. He tells us that inside the **MEMORY PALACE** is a sequence of bizarre scenes that connect in a way to help us remember some information that will get us the third and final piece to the key. He continues, saying that we need to pay attention because, at the end of it, we'll come across a large ferocious yeti who guards the gate that the key opens.

Sounds tough, but I'm confident in us. Your memory has been awesome so far. Rock-solid and strong. I'm so glad you agreed to go on this journey with me. Fingers crossed that we can continue past the next challenge!

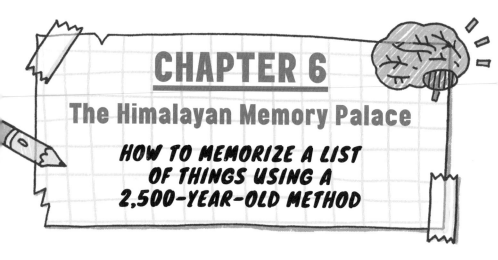

CHAPTER 6

The Himalayan Memory Palace

HOW TO MEMORIZE A LIST OF THINGS USING A 2,500-YEAR-OLD METHOD

Having just said goodbye to our new pirate friends and fresh off the boat, we lift our heads to look at the massive structure in front of us. Thirteen stories high and nearly a mile wide, this Tibetan palace is monstrous in size. One can only imagine how many hundreds of rooms are inside! I have no clue how we'll find our way through it, but we have to try and see what happens.

Somewhere inside this palace is the final piece to our key and we need to find it in order for our journey to continue. Once we do, the gate to the Himalayas (which is located at the back of the palace, I presume) will allow us to enter the Foreverest Valley. From there, we will trek all the way to base camp, where we will be able to stage our attempt to reach the summit of Mount Foreverest and, hopefully, defeat the Memory Thief.

I hate to tell you this, kid, but I don't know how much time my memory has left. I was useless in the desert, and even more useless on the pirate ship—I don't think I'll be much help from here on out. I've still got a few more awesome memory techniques to teach you before you'll be totally ready for the Memory Thief, so we better get moving on that before I completely forget *everything* I know!

What I'm going to teach you next is a technique that will . . . *Blow. Your. Mind.* It is one of the most powerful techniques out there and is the main method used by all expert memorizers for memorizing big things. Remember when I told you about the crazy memory feats I can do (or *could* do when my memory was intact), like memorizing a deck of cards in under a minute? Well, all of those feats were done using the technique I'm about to show you.

But first, a quick history lesson.

The famous story goes that, thousands of years ago, an ancient Greek poet named Simonides was having a big fancy dinner in his palace hall with all of his friends. He was suddenly called to meet with a messenger who had an important message for him, so he stepped away from his grand home. Tragically, the roof of the palace hall collapsed and buried everyone who was at the table, under the rubble. To remember all the guests and where they were sitting, Simonides had a clever idea: If he closed his eyes and thought back on the banquet table, he could remember them all as he went seat by seat around the table in his mind. It wasn't their faces he recalled; it was their *places*. And with that, he was able to name each of the guests who had been in that unfortunate accident. This was, as many say, the birth of the **MEMORY PALACE** technique.

The technique was then used by many civilizations over the years. Believe it or not, back then, memory was an art form. Being able to memorize was one of the most important skills to have. I mean, think

about it, there were no smartphones, no Google, no computers, not even any printed books—how else could information be shared between generations? By memory, of course. In schools, one of the first things that was taught was the art of memory, where teachers relayed to their students all the memory skills I've taught you. These were techniques that were constantly put to use throughout a person's life in order to remember speeches, texts, numbers, knowledge, and even sometimes the names of entire armies of soldiers.

With that story out of the way, I bet you're itching to know how to use the **MEMORY PALACE** technique, eh? It's very simple and it's quite similar to **THE PEG METHOD** we just learned. The method asks you to imagine a place you know very well (it can be your house, your school, the path you walk to *get* to school, or wherever you want), then to **LINK** the images of the things you're memorizing to locations (I call them "anchor points") along a path through that place. Similar to how we **LINK**ed images to letters of the alphabet with the Alphabet Peg List, but instead, we will be linking to a journey through some space.

This method is so powerful for one simple reason: Our brains are hardwired for it! We remember pictures and information about places and locations better than any other kind of information. So if we're going to memorize something, and we can turn them into pictures and store them in places, you're basically using **SEE-LINK-GO!** the exact way your brain likes it.

So, what do you say? Are you ready to take a walk through your first **MEMORY PALACE** journey?

Before we take a single step into this giant Himalayan **MEMORY PALACE**, I want to run you through an example of how the **MEMORY PALACE** technique works. For our first **MEMORY PALACE**, I'm going to use a place that both of us know *very, very* well: our own bodies.

NOTE TO READER

Memory palaces don't always have to be a physical structure like a house, apartment, or school. It really can be anything that takes up space and something you can create a path through that has a start and an end to it. You can make a path through your body, just like you can through your house. You can even create paths through scenes of a movie or even virtual worlds from video games you play (like the Fortnite map, perhaps?).

For a body memory palace, choose as many body parts as you like (these will be our "anchor points"), as long as they connect in some kind of order that is obvious and memorable. (Maybe start at your head and make your way down to your toes, or the other way around.) Let's jump right into an example that uses ten body parts to memorize ten things. How about the ten largest countries in the world by population?

Our ten body parts, starting at our heads, will be:

- TOP OF HEAD
- EARS
- EYES
- NOSE
- MOUTH
- CHIN
- ARMPITS
- BELLY BUTTON
- KNEES
- FEET

The ten countries are, in order, from most populated to least:

- **CHINA**
- **INDIA**
- **UNITED STATES**
- **INDONESIA**
- **BRAZIL**
- **PAKISTAN**
- **NIGERIA**
- **BANGLADESH**
- **RUSSIA**
- **JAPAN**

The first thing we need to do is to **SEE** the countries as images. Let's start with that:

CHINA The Great Wall of China

INDIA Taj Mahal

UNITED STATES Hamburger

INDONESIA Sounds like *in-dough-sneeze*-ia, so think of pressing *in* some *dough* with the palm of your hand, like a baker, and it causing you to *sneeze*

BRAZIL Soccer ball (since the Brazilian soccer team is so successful)

NIGERIA Sounds like Ni-*Cheerios* (close enough!)

PAKISTAN Sounds like a *pack* of cards *standing* on two little legs (*pack-i-stand*)

BANGLADESH Think of a gun going BANG! (*BANG*-ladesh)

RUSSIA Sounds like *rushing*. So a crosswalk with people *rushing* back and forth

JAPAN Imagine a cooking *pan* (Ja-*pan*)

Then we **LINK** and **GO!** using our body memory palace. Since the anchor points we're using are real things that are *actually* on our bodies, go ahead and imagine the images for each country interacting with your own body parts, as silly as that may sound!

● **TOP OF HEAD** The Great Wall of China is built right on top of your head, with the wall snaking around clumps of your hair.

● **EARS** Sticking out of both your ears are smaller replicas of the famous Taj Mahal building. That's got to be uncomfortable!

● **EYES** *PLOP!* An entire hamburger is dropped in place over your eye socket. Imagine a single tear of mayonnaise rolling down your cheek.

● **NOSE** Imagine pressing some dough into your nostrils, causing you to sneeze. ACHOO!

● **MOUTH** Imagine your mouth completely full of miniature soccer balls. You can't even speak, your mouth is so full!

● **CHIN** Resting on your chin is a full pack of cards standing on end. Maybe a card dealer is about to deal those standing cards straight from your chin!

● **ARMPITS** Cheerios are flying out of your armpits into a bowl for breakfast. Ew!

● **BELLY BUTTON** A bullet shoots out of your belly button like it's a gun—BANG!

● **KNEES** Your knees are now a busy crosswalk, painted black and white, with hundreds of people rushing over from one knee to the other. Back and forth they go!

● **FEET** Your feet are standing in a burning-hot pan, cooking your dinner. Your heels are even sizzling, causing you to have some nasty blisters.

There you have it. On your body, from head to toe, you now have all ten of the largest populated countries in order. Well done!

Here's a cool, little fun fact about memory palaces. You know when people say, "In the first place . . ." before they explain something? Well, that comes from long ago, when people were using the memory palace to help them remember a part of a speech. What they were doing when they said that was thinking about the first anchor point in their memory palace. In the "first place" of our recent body memory palace was the Great Wall of China, on your head!

Close your eyes and start at your head. See if you can remember all ten of the countries in order on your own! Now try it backward by starting at your feet instead!

Let's add a little extra something to the ten images on your body . . .

Remember that Great Wall on your HEAD? Make sure to add a very large, noticeable beige ring on top of it.

Those Taj Mahals coming out of your EARS? Imagine that, inside of those structures, there are some delicious sandwiches being made, making your ears the new deli spots on the street.

The burger on your EYE is washing a ton of tears out of your eyes.

Who's pressing in that dough on your NOSE and causing you to sneeze? Why, it's a jackrabbit driving a kart.

Imagine some bras that are silly on each of those soccer balls in your MOUTH.

On your CHIN, imagine that pack-of-standing-cards dealer asking you the question, "Is a llama bad?"

Those Cheerios coming out of your ARMPITS? Imagine a butcher chopping them up before they go in your cereal bowl.

For your BELLY button, imagine a duck coming out of there and shooting a gun—BANG! BANG!

KNEES—Instead of people rushing across that crosswalk, imagine some moss-covered cows. Mossy cows!

Imagine eating off that pan by your FEET and choking and saying, "YO!" to get someone's attention.

SURPRISE! YOU JUST MEMORIZED ALL THE CAPITALS FOR EACH OF THOSE COUNTRIES!

CHINA—beige ring = Beijing

INDIA—new deli = New Delhi

UNITED STATES—washing a ton = Washington, D.C.

INDONESIA—jackrabbit driving a kart = Jakarta

BRAZIL—bras silly = Brasilia

PAKISTAN—is a llama bad? = Islamabad

NIGERIA—a butcher = Abuja

BANGLADESH—duck = Dhaka

RUSSIA—a mossy cow = Moscow

JAPAN—Choke, yo! = Tokyo

See how we did that? We just slightly tweaked our original image by adding a tiny bit of extra detail to help us remember the capital. You can take this idea as far as you want. Maybe you want to add information about the population, a favorite national dish, whatever! You'll just add an extra image to your story for each location in your memory palace to help remember that extra fact. Pretty cool, right?

With that example out of the way, I think you're ready. Shall we enter the Memory Palace? I'm not sure what awaits us, but I would imagine we might be going from room to room witnessing some very strange scenes. Make sure to pay attention to each; you never know what kind of tests we might have to face at the end of it.

Here we go!

And with that, we both step into the palace.

Immediately in the first room, which is a big open hall decorated with dozens of Tibetan prayer wheels and flags, we encounter a large pack of **RESTING K-9** dogs with only two legs each. They look highly trained, so we better make sure not to wake them. They are resting and snoring, probably dreaming of chasing rabbits. We carefully tiptoe around them into the next room.

This next room is much smaller. It looks like a meditation room with a lot of monks in red robes quietly sitting with their eyes closed. In the opposite corner of the room, it's the famous Hong Kong–born action star Jackie Chan playing a game of Jenga. You have always wondered, **CAN CHAN JENGA?** Now you have your answer. Yes, he can! Out of nowhere, he starts yelling, "**LOT'S TO SEE! LOT'S TO SEE!**" like a crazy madman. (I guess he's trying to let us know that there's a lot to see in this massive Memory Palace . . . Thanks, Mr. Chan.) All the monks break from their meditative state and look angrily over at Jackie Chan. They're clearly not happy with him. We better move on before a fight breaks out!

We enter the next room and it's obviously a bathroom, with a man building a toilet by hand. He is **MAKING A LOO.** ("Loo" is the British way of saying "toilet," by the way.) As he's making this loo, he looks over at us and says in a very thick accent, "Lemme **CHO YOU.**" He comes over and leads us to the masterpiece that is a toilet. He clearly wants to show us this toilet of his. Thanks . . . but no thanks.

We're not that impressed, plus we have more important things to do than admire a handmade toilet. On to the next room, where we see a large open space with a **DOLLAR-CARRY**ing man who's flying around the room. This man is carrying stacks upon stacks of dollar bills on his back, while at the same time he is a **MAN WHO FLEW.** Interesting, and very bizarre, but still . . . We don't have time for this! On to the next room!

This next room is filled with golden statues and artwork. One work of art that is the focal point of the room is of a golfer putting a **MANGO** for **PAR** and using a baseball **BAT** as his club. We look at that sculpture for a few minutes, admiring its weirdness when, all of a sudden, we see something cross the canvas of a nearby painting—it's an **ANT BURNING!** This tiny ant is aflame, the poor guy. But the fire is getting larger, so we better go before the whole room burns down.

We rush out the back door and suddenly find ourselves face-to-face with a giant yeti guarding a large gate.

Wait, could this be it already? The gate to the Himalayas? Isn't this where we're supposed to use our key? But we still need the third piece! We must have skipped a room or three . . . Maybe we should go back . . .

"WHO GOES THERE?" the yeti booms.

"Uh . . . it's us . . . We're two explorers, trying to gain access to the Himalayas. May we pass?" I ask feebly.

"No, not unless you have the key. Do you have the key?" the yeti asks.

"Unfortunately, no, but we do have most of it. We are just missing a small piece of it . . ."

The yeti pulls out the third piece from behind him. "You mean this?" *GASP! He has the third piece!*

"I will give it to you. But you must be able to tell me what you saw in each of the five rooms you just walked through, from memory. Can you do that?" the yeti asks.

Gosh, *I* can't. I've forgotten it already. But can you?

You describe all five scenes to the yeti and he nods in approval.

"Well done!" He hands over the third piece. "Put all three key pieces together and then you may use it to open the gate behind me."

Trace back in your mind, starting at the beginning of the Memory Palace we just walked through (the "first place"), and see if you can remember what images you saw in each room. If you can't remember all of them, peek back and remind yourself, then try again.

Finally! We are one step closer to making it to the mountain. Are you excited? You did great remembering those Memory Palace rooms!

"Before you go," the yeti interrupts, "would you like to know what all those weird Memory Palace images meant?"

Sure, why not!

"They actually represent the ten highest mountains in the world (which are all in the Himalayan mountain range behind me, by the way)."

I know that some of the following mountain names are difficult. That's because they come from Nepal and Tibet, which is where these mountains are actually located in real life. Some of the images that were used in the rooms to represent the mountain names were single words, while others were a few words or even a phrase. This was done to help you remember the complicated mountain name.

EVEREST—*resting* (the dogs that were resting)

K2—*K-9* dogs with two legs

KANGCHENJUNGA—Remember we asked ourselves, "*Can* Jackie *Chan* play a game of *Jenga*?" (pronounced "can-chan-jenga")

LHOTSE—saying "*lots to see*" (pronounced just like that)

MAKALU—*making a loo* (pronounced "make-a-loo")

CHO OYU—saying "lemme *cho you*" (pronounced "cho you")

DHAULAGIRI—*Dollar-carry* (prounounced "dolla-gheeree")

MANASLU—Man who flew (pronounced "man-a-slew")

NANGA PARBAT—the painting with someone playing golf with a *mango* and getting *par* with a *bat*

ANNAPURNA—*ant burning* (pronounced "anna-per-na")

Wow! How cool is that? All we did was walk through a palace and see a few weird scenes in a few rooms and now we have ten *very* difficult mountain names stored in our memories (and in order, too)!

"Thanks, yeti. We'll be on our way now!" we say as we shake his furry hand. We take the third piece and add it to the other two and suddenly they all start glowing and it seems as if the etchings on the metal surface have come alive. After unlocking the gate with our now whole key, we push it open to reveal the stunning Foreverest Valley ahead of us filled with countless snowcapped mountains as far as the eye can see.

We take our first steps into the lush gorge. I have a feeling this journey is about to get way more intense!

NOTE TO READER

You can create as many memory palaces as you like. The more the better, allowing you to store more things! Creating memory palaces is as simple as sitting down and thinking of a place you know, and then thinking of a path through it. Each point along the path (or anchor point) is a storage spot for a piece of information. So the more of those you have, the more you can store. I get asked a lot how many palaces I keep for my memory training. The answer is hundreds! And each one has many different anchor points. With them, I've been able to memorize hundreds of cards, thousands of digits, really long written texts, and more. And if I ever run out of memory palaces, I just think of more. It's easy!

Come up with your own memory palaces to use for things you need every day. Maybe you can use one to remember the homework assignments you need to get done. Or maybe to remember things your teacher says. It's up to you!

Start by thinking of places that you know really well and think of paths leading through them. On those paths, choose anchor points along the way. (Those will be the things you LINK your images to—they can be anything: a piece of furniture, a wall, a corner, an entire room, whatever you feel like.) Make sure that your path makes sense, too. Don't jump from the front door to the backyard to the kitchen, for example. Make your path go in a direction that makes sense in real life.

Then, think of something challenging that you'd like to memorize. Something fun. Maybe all of the Pokémon or all of the NFL Super Bowl champions in history.

Finally, create a memory palace large enough to hold each piece of information and try to challenge yourself to memorize it all. It may not happen in a day, but you could work on it over a few days or weeks.

NOTE TO READER

Can you reuse memory palaces? Yes, you can. But you run the risk of maybe confusing what you want to remember with things you remember from a time you used it before. So, here's my advice: If you're memorizing something you'd like to keep forever, create a new memory palace and use it only for that information—nothing else. I memorized all the Best Picture winners from the Oscars and I used a specific memory palace that was only used for that task. But then for everyday things that I only need to remember for a short time, I might reuse specific memory palaces.

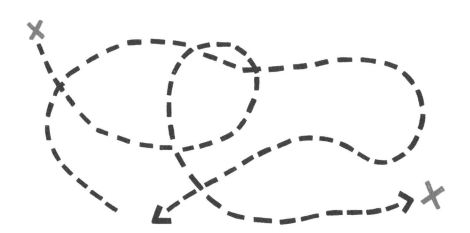

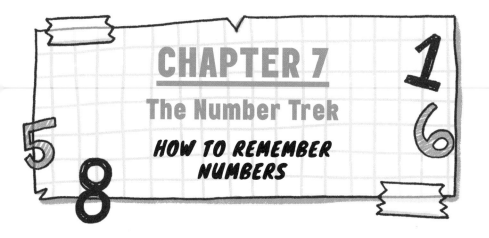

CHAPTER 7
The Number Trek
HOW TO REMEMBER NUMBERS

After a few hours of trekking through the Foreverest Valley, we start to notice something very strange. Looking around, we realize that numbers are *everywhere*. How did we miss that? They were scribbled all over the trekking path, etched into rocks that we passed, and wrapped around the handrails of rope bridges that we crossed. There were even animals that we passed that were in the *shape* of numbers; that was the craziest of them all! I mean, look at that yak over there for example. I think that's a yak, right? But it's in the shape of a big sideways 3. Ha!

This hike has been stunningly beautiful so far, starting in the lower altitudes of the valley, where fields were teeming (remember that word?) with lush, green trees and bushes, but now the scenery is becoming more rugged and rocky at the higher elevations. And the farther up we go, there are even more numbers surrounding us.

As gorgeous as all the scenery is here, and as much bizarro stuff as we've seen on our journey so far, this number business pretty much takes the cake for *weirdest thing ever*. Numbers, numbers, numbers. That's all we see for *miles*. I'm starting to get the impression that this part of our journey is going to have a lot to do with digits. In which case, I better get started teaching you some ways to memorize them. And my memory is getting worse by the minute, so let's hurry.

In real life, just like this valley, numbers are actually everywhere when you think about it. They're in every sport you watch or play, in your multiplication tables at school, and even in the graphics of your favorite video game. But no matter how much they show up in our lives, a lot of people feel that they are "bad at math" or "bad with numbers." This feeling is something I like to call *number sense*, and a lot of people don't have it! If you aren't familiar with numbers—if numbers aren't your friends—then your number sense isn't going to be very strong and memorizing numbers is going to be extremely difficult.

So how do we make numbers friendly?

Numbers are symbols. And symbols don't mean much to people. That's why people don't have good number sense—that's why numbers aren't friendly! If you've learned anything up to now, it's that *all* information that we see, hear, feel, touch, or smell are symbols. They only make sense to us when we give them meaning. And when something makes sense to us, it feels good and familiar like an old friend, right?

Some things are easier to give meaning to than others, like a simple noun, a person's name you recognize, or a picture of something you've seen before, just to name a few. For example, think of an *elephant*. I bet that was super easy to do, wasn't it? That's because when you read the word e-l-e-p-h-a-n-t, all those letters squashed together, you instantly see a picture in your mind of a humongous gray animal with a long trunk and white tusks. You probably learned what "elephant" meant by the time you were three, having watched them in a cartoon or seen them at the zoo. Here's another example: Think of a *xylango*.

AHA! Is your brain as empty as a coconut right now? You probably couldn't think of one, right? It's not your fault . . . because a xylango doesn't exist. I made it up! But who knows, maybe they *do* exist and we've just never seen any or learned about them. We've never learned that the letters x-y-l-a-n-g-o together mean something. In any case, a xylango is unfamiliar to us, and so we can't picture it or give it any meaning.

It's the same with numbers. What does 541246 mean to you? Anything? Probably not. And that's okay. To a lot of people, it just looks like six random number symbols stuck together and nothing more than that. But what if I told you, that for me, it means a *horse solving a Rubik's cube made out of mushrooms*? That's what I **SEE** when I read that specific six-digit number.

Um . . . why does it mean that? I'm sure you're asking, and you'll understand soon, but the point I'm trying to make here is that numbers are hard because they are difficult to **SEE** . . . difficult to give meaning. My task in this chapter is to teach you a few different ways to go about **SEE**ing numbers as pictures—to make numbers more familiar to you, and hopefully make them your new best friends (after me, of course)! We're going to use something I like to call *number systems* to do that. I'm about to make you a number genius. By the end of this chapter, your number sense will be shooting through the roof, and you'll have amazing number-memorizing superpowers!

Let's start with small numbers. By small numbers, I mean single digits: 0, 1, 2, 3, 4, 5, 6, 7, 8, and 9. Every number in the universe can be made up of just those ten things. The number 24? That's just a 2 and a 4 together. The number 23,588? That's just a 2, 3, 5, 8, and another 8 together. If we can find a picture for each of those ten digits—a picture that stands for each digit *every* time we see it—then we'll be able to **SEE** any number. And if we can do that, then we can *memorize* any number we want.

The first two number systems I'm going to teach you are the Number-Rhyme System and the Number-Shape System. The names of those systems give you a good idea of what they do. For the Number-Rhyme System, we will come up with a word that *rhymes* with each digit. For the Number-Shape System, we will come up with an object that each digit's *shape* looks like. Simple enough, right?

Here are the images that I use for the Rhyme System:

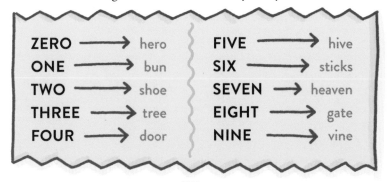

And here are the images for the Shape System:

0. BALL (any round object) examples: tennis ball, gum ball, marble, etc.

1. STICK (any stick-shaped object) examples: baseball bat, pencil, knife, etc.

2. SWAN (any type of bird with a long neck) examples: swan, duck, goose, etc.

3. BUTTERFLY (or any type of insect) examples: ant, cockroach, beetle, etc.

4. SAILBOAT (any boat) examples: sailboat, yacht, cruise ship, etc.

5. SNAKE (any reptile/ animal) examples: snake, worm, salamander, turtle, etc.

6. GOLF CLUB (any sports racket, club, device) examples: golf club, field hockey stick, tennis racket, etc.

7. BOOMERANG (any object with a single bend) examples: boomerang, arrowhead, shelf bracket, etc.

8. SNOWMAN (anything snow-related, Christmassy) examples: snowman, reindeer, Santa, etc.

9. FLAGPOLE or **BALLOON ON A STRING** (anything like a stick with an object on the end of it) examples: flagpole, balloon on a string, hot-air balloon, etc.

NOTE TO READER

These images are just suggestions. If you don't like them, or if you don't like the way they make you feel, make up your own! BUT a word of caution: Don't just come up with anything you like. There needs to be a reason why you came up with it. These systems are designed to help you remember numbers more easily. So if you forget why a number stood for a picture you made up, then you're just making it more difficult for yourself. Bottom line: Make your reason for the image obvious and easy (oh, and fun!).

The Rhyme System images should make sense (they all rhyme!). But for some of the Shape System images, you might not be sure why I chose them. Remember, it's all about the shape; things that the digit looks like. Why a swan for 2? Well, a 2 looks a bit like a peaceful swan floating on a pond, don't you think? Why a butterfly for 3? It looks like half of a butterfly wing. A snake for 5? Imagine a rattlesnake perched and ready to bite. You get the idea. And notice that I keep it pretty vague. 0 can be any round-shaped object. I do that so I have a lot of freedom when thinking of my images. If I have a bunch of zeros in a row, it will be more memorable to have a bunch of different round objects than just the same exact ball, one after the other.

Once you've learned these number systems (you can use either one), if you want to memorize some digits, all you have to do is **LINK** your images for the numbers using one of the methods we already know (Story Method, word association, Peg Method, or Memory Palace), and then **GO!**

RHYME SYSTEM

SHAPE SYSTEM

Now, which **LINK** method you use depends on how long the number is and what it's being used for—is it for a math equation? A short code? Someone's phone number? If the number is short enough, using the Rhyme or Shape System is perfect. But if the number gets too long, then with just single-digit images, you're going to end up with a lot of images to remember! For bigger numbers, you're better off with a more powerful system. We want memorizing to be easy, don't we?

Before we move on to that, let's hang to the side and take a rest. This high altitude can make us light-headed and thirsty, so let's have a seat and refuel.

We plop down on a nearby rock and drink a few sips from our water bottles. As we take in the beautiful nature around us (covered in numbers, of course), we notice a few strange things happening on a rope bridge not too far away. We see a:

. . . snowman holding a snake, which is hissing at a butterfly, who is landing on another snowman . . .

Funny we should see that; it reminds you of our number system, doesn't it? What would that silly image be as a number using our Number-Shape System?

See if you can remember what each image was as a digit and say the whole number. Can you do it? (Peek back a couple of pages if you need a hint!)

That exact string of images on the bridge stands for an exact sequence of digits. Cool, right? The story could have also easily been *a gate with bee-hives all over it, and the bees fly over to a tree which also has a gate.* (That's the same number as above, but with the images from the Number-Rhyme System. In the end, it doesn't matter which system you use. Choose one if you like it better than the other. Or use both whenever you feel like it. No worries!

Let's say that the number you wanted to memorize was longer than the example we just did. You could always just create one long story using **THE STORY METHOD**, but that could get confusing. Instead, you could break the big number up into smaller groups, a few digits at a time, and store each little chunk on different anchors in a memory palace or on some pegs. Or if a number represented a year or a date, and you wanted to remember some historical event that happened in that year, you could use the word association method we learned earlier.

Oh, hey! Look over there!

On a different bridge we see a *pencil* stabbing an *orange* and then two *golf clubs* whacking them to pieces. Make sure to notice that this scene we just saw was a *battle* and that it happened quickly . . . or *hastily.*

WHACK!

It may not be obvious, but that little group of images is the year of the *Battle of Hastings* (a very important battle in British history). It happened in the year *1066*. Think of all the shapes: pencil–orange–golf club–golf club—that's 1-0-6-6. And we associated it to *battle* and *hastily*. See what we did there? We converted our numbers into pictures and then **LINK**ed it to another picture (the name of the battle) to help us remember that the number, or year, went with a historical event. That's the exact same thing we did in chapter 4, with all those examples in the desert, only this time with a bit of numbers mixed in.

You can also use this method to remember a short code . . . like, say, the pin code to open your parent's phone? It's usually a short, four-digit number, right? Check this out:

● Let's say the number to unlock your parent's cell phone is 1002.

Let's use the Rhyme System to keep things interesting. 1 is a bun—maybe a soggy, moldy hamburger bun that no one wants to eat. 0 is a hero—how about your favorite superhero? The second 0 is another big and beefy hero. And the 2 is a shoe—a big, stinky ol' basketball shoe. Our story will be as follows: You're sitting down for a nice afternoon snack and you pick up a really gross, soggy, moldy hamburger. YUCK! You can't eat that or you'll get really sick, so a nearby hero—with his senses tingling—shoots the burger away from your mouth. Not only that, but a big and beefy superhero barges in to punch that burger into the sky. But the force of that punch knocks your oversized, stinky sneakers right off your feet!

We're not done yet; we still have to attach that image to the cell phone somehow (to remind you that the number is the code for your parent's phone). So imagine that this bizarre story is now one of the most viral videos of our time, gaining over one billion views in just a few minutes! Everyone can't stop watching it! Now imagine seeing this bizarre viral video on your parent's phone.

Well, how about that? You just memorized the code *forever*.

Let's try something else. How about a few tricky multiplication table problems? Ooh, I know you don't like those, do you? A lot of people forget 8 x 8, and 6 x 7, so let's try our method on those, to see if we can cement them in our heads forever.

● 8 x 8 = 64

An 8 in my Shape System is a snowman. Since it's 8 x 8, I'll picture two *snowmen* on the left side. On the right side of the times table fact is 64. I'm going to take a little shortcut. 64 instantly means something to me. It reminds me of *Nintendo 64*! I used to play that gaming system when I was younger—boy, does that bring back some happy memories! So let's **LINK** the two sides of this equation. I have *two snowmen playing Nintendo 64 with each other*. BOOM! Simple as that. Memorable!

NOTE TO READER

If a number (no matter how long it is) means something to you already (maybe it's your birthday or it's a lyric from a song you like), use that image! Don't waste time turning all those digits into shapes or rhymes. We're all about saving time!

● 6 x 7 = 42

A 6 is a *golf club* and a 7 is a *boomerang*. I'm going to imagine a *golf club* whacking a *boomerang* across a field. After a while, it lands on a *sailboat* (4) that has a *swan* (2) as a captain. There you have it! 6 x 7 is equal to that 4 and 2: 42!

136

QUICK REMINDER: Don't forget to really GO! when you're thinking of these images. That's really the step that's going to cause these images to be so sticky you can't forget them. I'm writing them out quickly for you in these examples because by now I know you're a pro and that you're remembering to add that special sauce to make these images go *UMPH* and stick better!

Multiplication tables are tough to memorize because there are so many problems to remember and a lot of them look very similar. If you take the time to write down the ones that give you a hard time and come up with images for them like we just did, you'll be memorizing those guys in no time! If you need some help, you can view one of my online videos.

Remember back in chapter 5 when I mentioned being able to use numbers as a peg list? Well, now you have images for numbers, so you can use them as a peg list. Just like you attached an image of something you wanted to memorize to each letter of the alphabet, you can now do that to each digit image. Let's say the first thing on a list you want to memorize is the word *milk*. I could imagine *milk* being poured all over a burger bun (bun = 1). Then the next item on my list would stick on a shoe (shoe = 2). And so on.

All right, water break's over. Let's get a move on. After a few more bridges, we're going to pass into a clearing—a plateau—which is surrounded by all the massive peaks in the Himalayas. From there Mount Foreverest will finally be in plain view. Before we get there, I want to show you an even more powerful number system called the Major System. The Number-Rhyme System and the Number-Shape System are great for thinking of images for numbers super quickly, but the Major System will allow you to be able to memorize ANY SIZE NUMBER YOU WANT! (I even used it to memorize 10,000 digits once . . . that's one *thousand* phone numbers! Holy Batman!) Also, when using the Rhyme or Shape System frequently, you're often going to find yourself dealing with a lot of repeat images (you might end up seeing loads of snowmen and butterflies for instance, if the number has a lot of 8's and 3's in it). The Major System gets rid of this problem almost entirely.

To become really good at memorizing numbers, you need to be able to read them as easily as you read words. If you can find a way to turn numbers into words just by quickly reading them, then you'll be able to remember bigger numbers, fast. The Major System is your best bet—and it only takes a few minutes to learn!

Here's how it works.

The idea of the Major System is to turn every digit of a number into a consonant sound. By connecting those consonant sounds and stuffing any vowels that make sense in between those consonants, you can create words. Once you have words, it's just like memorizing anything else!

I know numbers can seem hard, but honestly, the hardest part of this system is remembering which consonants represent which numbers—and they're actually a breeze to learn. Watch! Here are the ten digits and the consonant sounds they represent. I'll share a quick mnemonic to help you remember each one:

0 = s, z, or soft c (as in "cider")—the z in "zero" should make you think of the sound.

1 = t or d—both t and d require you to write one downstroke when you write them, which looks like the number 1. T and d also share a similar sound.

2 = n—because n has two downstrokes.

3 = m—because m has three downstrokes. (Also, flip that 3 over and you've got an m!)

4 = r—the last letter of four is r.

5 = L—if you hold up your left hand, which has five fingers, the shape between your pointer finger and thumb makes an L shape.

6 = j, sh, soft g (as in "ginger"), or soft ch (as in "change")—6 is like a lowercase g rotated 180 degrees; sh, j, and soft ch are lumped together because they sound similar.

7 = K, hard c (as in "cash"), hard g (as in "gamble"), ck, q—the capital K, when rotated 90 degrees clockwise, looks like two mirror images of 7's back-to-back. See it?

8 = f or v—the cursive lowercase f looks like an 8; f and v have similar sounds.

9 = p or b—9 looks like a mirror image of p, which looks like an upside-down lowercase b.

Okay, so now what?

To take a number and turn it into a word based on the *phonetic code* we just learned (*phonetic* is a fancy word meaning "having to do with how something sounds"), simply study the number and figure out which consonant sounds the numbers represent. At this point, you won't have a word; it will just be a mash-up of consonants (and not that memorable). The next step is to squeeze in some vowels wherever you like and feel is appropriate to turn that mush of consonants into an actual real word! Think of it like this: Vowels are free, and consonant sounds stand for numbers. You can use vowels wherever you want because they don't stand for any numbers. Also, since it's a system based on *sounds* (phonetic, remember?), the spelling doesn't really matter, either.

As we trek along this path toward Mount Foreverest, let me show you some examples of how to convert some numbers into words using the Major System.

Look over there: See that big 86 scratched into the boulder? Let's turn that into a word.

 86

First, let's turn these two digits into their possible consonant sounds (there are a few choices). The basic breakdown is:

8   **6**
(F or V) + (J or SH or G or CH)

How can we fill in the gaps with vowels to make it into a real word? Let's play around with our options a bit. There are a few combinations, but how about: FOG or FISH? I like FISH, because it's an easy word to imagine.

There you have it 86 = FISH. That big number 86 on the boulder is turning into a big, colorful, smelly FISH, flopping about. That's way easier than remembering 86.

When you're trying to remember your numbers later on and you think of an image of a FISH, thinking back to the Major System code; you'll pick out those consonant sounds (F and SH) and turn them back into digits—8 and 6 . . . 86!

This may feel a *bit* challenging, I know. But if you've ever had to learn a language, you know that it takes practice. This is a *number* language. You have to use it again and again for it to become super easy. So, with a bit of practice, reading numbers as words, and words as numbers, you'll get there.

Oh, look over there at that raven flying overhead. It's got the number 35 on its side made by colored feathers. Let's try to convert that number, too:

35 breaks down to:

$$\textbf{3} \qquad \textbf{5}$$
$$\text{(M)} + \text{(L)}$$

We can insert some vowels in and around those letters for a few choice options of words: MAIL, MALE, MOLE, EMAIL, MILE, MULE . . . You get the idea. I like MAIL. Instead of that raven flying around, now it's a clunky MAILbox.

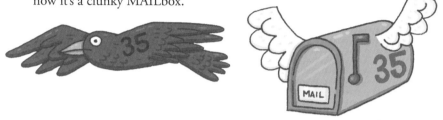

And that tree over there? It's got 27's written all over it. How would we convert that one?

27 breaks down to:

2   **7**
(N) + (K or C or G or CKor Q)

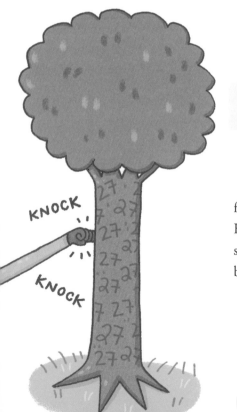

NAG, NICK, KNOCK (that first K is silent, so it's okay). I like KNOCK. Imagine a KNOCKing sound whenever you KNOCK on the bark of that tree.

KNOCK

KNOCK

One last one. See that 323 written on the path?

 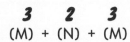 **323**

Going up to a three-digit number, 323 breaks down to:

$$3 \quad 2 \quad 3$$
$$(M) + (N) + (M)$$

The larger the number gets, the more difficult it is to find one single word. Try your best, but if you can't, just break it down into multiple words and **LINK** those words together. With these consonants, we have: AMMONIUM (the double M just counts as one single M sound, so no worries). Or even simpler, how about the yummy candy M&M's? There are now MNMs scattered all the way down this path. YUM!

Here are a few numbers and words for you to try and translate. Check out the Appendix for the answers once you're done!

• 68

• 71

• 18

• RAT

• PUKE

• SPELL

• SPAGHETTI
(This is a tough one! Just sound it out!)

Numbers are everywhere, so if you want to practice more, try finding numbers around you and converting them into words. License plates, phone numbers, codes, whatever! They're all over! And the more you practice thinking in this number language, the better you'll get at it.

Now that you have this phonetic code locked in your brain, let's look at how to use it for longer numbers. Think back for a second—earlier in this book, I mentioned something called *chunking*. Remember that? That's where we take many things and *chunk* them into one single (or smaller) thing. Numbers are perfect for chunking because many numbers in real life are long (phone numbers, passport numbers, answers to math problems, etc.), and remembering one short thing is way easier than remembering a long thing. Using the Major System, we can chunk a few digits at a time into words.

Let's try a few fun examples, so you get the idea.

● Tallest building in the world: Burj Khalifa, 2,717 feet high.

Here we have one of those chapter 4 equations, right? Burj Khalifa = 2717. Let's start with the number. We could use the Number-Shape or Number-Rhyme system since it's a small enough number, but let's use the Major System so you get a feel for how it works as well. Coming up with a word for 2717 (four digits) might be a challenge. But let's try.

2717 breaks down to:

2   **7**   **1**   **7**
(N) + (K or C or G or CK or Q) + (T or D) + (K or C or G or CK or Q)

Hmm . . . that's tough. I can't think of any. But that's okay. This can happen. What usually is easier, is to break the number into smaller chunks. Let's break it into two words. One for 27 and one for 17, then we can connect them.

27 breaks down to:

2   **7**
(N) + (K or C or G or CK or Q)

We used KNOCK before, so let's stick with that.

17 breaks down to:

1   **7**
(T or D) + (K or C or G or CK or Q)

Let's use DOG.

So, we have KNOCK-DOG for the large number 2717. Imagine knocking a dog over on its side. Sooo mean! Why would you do that? For Burj Khalifa (which is a tough pair of words), it makes me think of *bridge cauliflower*. (It's not a perfect translation, but close enough to how it sounds.) Let's imagine a bridge made of cauliflower and you try knocking a dog off of it. Nice!

● **A phone number: 555-291-8023**

Something a bit longer this time. Ten digits! To be safe, since I don't know how big a chunk of numbers I can create words from, let's group the area code in a group of three, then the next three, and then split up the last four in two and two.

555 breaks down to:

> **5   5   5**
> (L) + (L) + (L)

How about LALALA (like someone singing)?

291 breaks down to:

> **2   9   1**
> (N) + (P or B) + (T or D)

That works out nicely to NAPPED.

80 breaks down to:

$$\underset{\text{(F or V)}}{\textbf{\textit{8}}} \quad \underset{\text{(S or Z)}}{\textbf{\textit{0}}}$$

That's FIZZY. Like a FIZZY soda drink.

23 breaks down to:

$$\underset{\text{(N)}}{\textbf{\textit{2}}} \quad \underset{\text{(M)}}{\textbf{\textit{3}}}$$

That's NOM. Like what you say when you're hungry and eating something delicious: NOM-NOM-NOM.

So all together we have LALALA-NAPPED-FIZZY-NOM. For fun, let's use a number shape peg list to store each word in order! LALALA goes with a *ball* (for 0, the first number on our peg list). NAPPED goes with a *stick*. FIZZY goes with a *swan*. And NOM goes with *butterfly*. So imagine these:

- Imagine someone singing LALALA really loud at a *ball*. So loud, even, that it explodes . . . KABLOW!

- Think of a *stick* that just NAPPED. He was *just* snoozing, zzzZZZZ, and now he is awake.

- Think of a **FIZZY** *swan*. This swan is just floating on a pond, fizzing up like a fizzy drink.

- Imagine **NOM-NOM-NOM**ing on a delicious *butterfly*.

There you have it. Now, to remember the number, just go through your peg list from 0 to however many you used and translate the words back to numbers!

Let's do one more. A historical event again, but this time with the full date!

November 6, 1860—Abraham Lincoln is elected president.

The year 1860 can be turned into TOUGH-SHOES if I split it into 2's (18-60). Picture a really TOUGH, sturdy pair of SHOES being thrown at Abraham Lincoln as he wins the election, taking the stage for his presidential victory speech.

Now what do we do about the month and date? November is the eleventh month of the year and we have the sixth day of the month. 11 turns into TOT (like a delicious, crunchy, piping-hot, ketchup-slathered, tater TOT). And 6 turns into SHY. (It's just that one consonant sound SH, plus any extra vowel sounds I want.)

So now, instead of just those TOUGH-SHOES being thrown at Honest Abe, it's a tater TOT that is SHY, quietly and carefully throwing some TOUGH-SHOES at Abe Lincoln during his victory speech. Picturing that just makes me LOL. Ha ha!

See if you can come up with your own memorable images for these important historical dates:

1905—Einstein writes physics paper

1885—First car is built

1953—First Mount Everest summit

2007—First iPhone released

You can see how I memorized these in the Appendix.

The clearing! It's up ahead!

A few steps up the final part of the hill and past a few more big boulders, and then we find ourselves able to see dozens of gigantic peaks towering over us and all around. We pause. Looking up at them, the routes to the summit on each of them seem treacherous, cold, and scary. So much snow and rock. Makes you wonder what it's like up there . . .

I point to the tallest mountain straight ahead of us.

"There she is!" I say. "Mount Foreverest! What a beauty . . ."

Our final objective is right there in front of us. Hard to believe that after this whole journey, we're finally getting there. As we continue on, we notice some very distinct numbers outlined in a bright yellow color on the pebble stones of the pathway. 3, 1, 4, 1 . . . the number reads.

"This number looks really long . . . but important. Let's memorize it, just in case. Using the Major System again, we can create words as we go. Since we're pressed for time, let's use **THE STORY METHOD** to connect it all in a story really quickly."

As we go along the path, these are the numbers we see:

● 3.14159265358979323846

WOOF. That's long, eh? But, hmm . . . That number looks a bit familiar. It's the famous mathematical constant named *pi*. You might have learned about this number a little bit when you were covering shapes, circles, and geometry. Most people only know 3.14, but wow, *twenty-one* digits of pi? That's a lot. Hopefully, with the Major System, it should be a breeze.

Let's start right after the decimal point since we know pi starts with "three point . . ." I think we should pair two digits at a time as we create words, what do you think?

Okay, if we do that, we will get the following words:

14 = TIRE	**35** = MULE	**79** = CAPE
15 = DOLL	**89** = FIB	**32** = MOON
92 = PEN	(FIB is a another word for "lie")	**38** = MOVIE
65 = JELLO		**46** = RASH

Now the easy part: Just **LINK** and **GO!**

Try to link all these words together using **THE STORY METHOD.** Make sure to make your story as vivid and silly as possible! You can see the story I chose in the Appendix.

After reading the last digit on the path and having memorized the whole thing with our number system, we bump right into a herd of hairy, mooing yaks (yaks in the shape of numbers. Remember we saw one like these earlier?) and a yak herder guiding them along. They seem harmless enough, but the yaks are surrounding us and we can't get out. They're too big and heavy to move! Uh-oh . . .

"You can only pass if you give me the twenty-one-digit number you just saw along the path," the yak herder explains to us. "It is the code I created to make sure anyone who walks toward Mount Foreverest is ready to face the mountain. You must recite the number from memory, and only then will I allow you to pass. Mount Foreverest Base Camp is just down the way over there. I'm guessing you're heading there . . . So tell me the number and I will let you through . . ."

Do you remember what the twenty-one digits are? I for sure don't. My memory is in bad shape right now. It's all on you, my friend. Give it a shot!

Try to recite all twenty-one of the first digits of pi from memory! If you're brave enough, do it in front of your friends to impress them.

You shout out all of the twenty-one digits in perfect order.

"THAT IS CORRECT!" the yak herder tells us excitedly. "You are ready for the mountain. You may pass!" He shoos away all of the yaks to reopen the pathway before us.

Wow, *great* job again! You are really mastering these memorizing superpowers. Keep this up and the Memory Thief won't stand a chance!

As we pass the herd of yaks, grunting at us as we walk by, the mountain continues to loom overhead. As we approach it, getting closer and closer, the immense shadow from the peak begins to blanket us. It almost feels like nighttime, with the peak nearly blocking out the sun completely. We squint our eyes to try and see the very top of the peak, to see if we can maybe catch a small glimpse of the evil Memory Thief. But no luck. It's too high up. One can *only* imagine the dangers up there that await us . . .

NOTE TO READER

If you want to become a number-memorizing master like me (well, before my memory started to disappear), I would suggest pre-learning images for all of the two-digit combinations from 00 to 99. If you do this, no matter how big of a number you come across, you can always break it up into twos. Then you can store pairs of images in locations through a memory palace.

Let's say you wanted to memorize 12345678901234567890 (stupid number, I know, but just for example). If you had your Major System learned, you would read it as 12-34-56-78-90-12-34-56-78-90. Then you would group the images for 12-34 in the first room of your memory palace, 56-78 in the next, and so on. It's easier to do it this way because it makes memorizing numbers the same *every time*. Which makes numbers feel like your best, best friends. And that's the goal, isn't it?

To see my full Major System for all two-digit numbers, look at the Appendix. A small word of warning: It does take a bit of time to learn all of them. But, if you do, they stick with you for life!

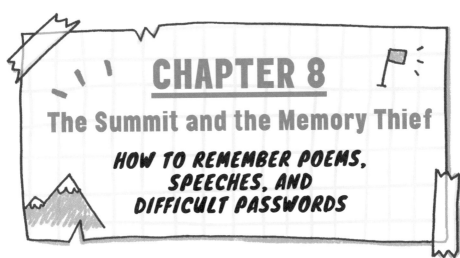

CHAPTER 8

The Summit and the Memory Thief

HOW TO REMEMBER POEMS, SPEECHES, AND DIFFICULT PASSWORDS

We step into base camp, a mile-long stretch of small peaks and valleys of rock and ice, slowly curving into the mouth of the bottom ice glacier of Mount Foreverest herself—the majestic beast of a mountain. The mountain of never forgetting and remembering forever. Or, well, at least it used to be known as that before the Memory Thief took up residence there and started stealing everyone's memories.

We set up our camp for the night: pitching our tent, boiling some water, and heating up soup, then getting all nestled into our cozy sleeping bags. The temperature outside is bone-chilling, but inside our tent, it's nice and warm. We'll be able to get some much-needed rest after all of our recent adventures. And as unusual as our adventures have been so far, I suspect that it's going to get even more crazy on the upper slopes of this mountain.

We say good night to each other and begin counting yaks. (Out here, we count yaks, not sheep.)

Zzzzz . . .

Before we know it, the sun is filling our tent with light. It's time to get up and get moving.

THIS. IS. IT.

Finally, the moment of truth. All the memory superpowers I've taught you to this point on our journey are about to be put to the test. Up until now, you've been learning the basics bit by bit. You've learned how to tackle a lot of the kinds of things you might see and learn at school in nice bite-sized pieces. But today, our last challenge will be to memorize a mixture of things, both easy and hard, all mashed up together.

I've actually known that we would face something like this from the very beginning of our journey, but was waiting to tell you about it until I knew whether or not you would be able to handle it. You definitely have proved that you can.

I know the secret to defeating the Memory Thief. The Memory Thief's weakness is threefold: a speech recited from memory, remembering math equations, and worst of all, keeping track of complicated passwords.

How funny is that? He steals all of our memories, but the few things that he can't stand are memorized text, formulas, and passwords? That's hilarious.

So you know what that means, don't you? It means that you'll have to memorize examples of those three things as we climb up the slopes of Mount Foreverest, using all the techniques you've learned so far, and then recite them on the summit to the face of the Memory Thief. Fingers crossed, but hopefully it destroys him and everyone's memories are restored—mine included. Speaking of my memory, I can feel it slipping away from me more and more; as if I have just a number of hours left before everything will go completely gone. We need to really move now . . .

Luckily, I managed to peek a glance at a map of the mountain back in the Himalayan Memory Palace. It was hanging on the wall in the last room with all that strange artwork. I can't remember everything about it, but what I *do* recall is that it showed there were three main features on the mountain that we would need to pass through in order to gain access to the summit:

● **The Speechless Icefall**

● **The Equation Cwm (pronounced "coom")**

● **The Password Wall**

First, at the bottom of the mountain, just outside of base camp, is the mouth of the glacier. This is the Speechless Icefall. An icefall is one of the most treacherous parts of a mountain. It is where all the snow and ice from the top of the mountain meets the valley floor. On the mountain, gravity pulls things down ever so slowly. Over hundreds of years this pileup of snow and ice has turned into a popcorn maze of massive ice blocks and crevasses. Once there, we'll have to navigate *very* carefully so

as not to fall in or get injured. I wasn't able to learn everything about this section of the mountain, but it seems to me that there will be some sort of a speech we will see along the way that we'll have to memorize.

Second, once we pass that section, we'll enter the Equation Cwm—a cwm is a steep-sided valley in between mountainsides, in case you didn't know. We'll have to navigate through that space to get to the next section. In the cwm, we'll encounter one large mathematical equation, which we'll have to . . . yep, memorize as well.

Finally, once through that, we'll reach the base of the Password Wall—a sheer ice wall, rising nearly three thousand feet to the last summit pyramid of the mountain. This face is so steep, we'll need to use our ropes to anchor in to different ice anchors that are bolted into the mountain as we make our way up. At each anchor, we will learn one new character symbol, which will be part of a long and uncrackable password. No doubt we will have to memorize that as well.

One slip anywhere on this part of the mountain will be fatal and our expedition will be over. So be extra careful, think about the techniques I've taught you, use everything you've learned during our entire journey, and make sure you get everything in your head before we reach the summit. I need not remind you, but I won't be able to help you much along the way. Maybe a few suggestions here and there, but all the memorization will be up to you. Got it?

We've got no time to spare. Let's get climbing. Strap on your harness, put on your crampons, tie in to this rope, and let's start moving up this mountain PRONTO.

We navigate our way through the maze of rock and ice that lies immediately outside our campsite. At first, it's just a very gradual incline; nothing too dangerous. But after about thirty minutes, we reach a big wooden sign that tells us we are at the start of the Speechless Icefall:

Clipping our rope into the first anchor, we begin our first challenge. Into the icefall we go . . .

In our age of PowerPoint presentations, flash cards, and even good old ink and paper, we easily forget that memory techniques were once the only way for people to deliver speeches. The ancient Greeks mastered these thousands of years ago, but nowadays it has mostly been forgotten. In school, when your teacher made you memorize a poem, or when you were in a school play and had to recite line after line, or when you had to give a big speech about a topic you researched, you probably memorized it by going over it again and again. That's called *rote memorization* (remember?) and it's *completely* the wrong way to use your memory. Sure, it eventually works, but it takes way too much time and it's not always reliable. Memorizing text is hard, I get it—because it's filled with so many words, tons of little details, complicated words, easy words, sometimes even foreign words and numbers—but you should know by now that you can make just about *any* piece of information easily memorable by using **SEE-LINK-GO!** All you'll have to do is bring all your memory skills together in order to memorize it.

Let's start with a technique that will help you memorize a short piece of text. It can work for longer texts, too, but it works best with text that is just a few sentences at a time. This technique works like magic and will completely blow you away once you try it. I call it the First Letter Method. While it's very simple, it won't make things stick forever *unless* you pair it with one of the **LINK** steps you've already learned. Either way, it's a great first step to getting a bunch of difficult words into your memory insanely fast. And once it's in your memory, you can then apply **SEE-LINK-GO!** at your own pace.

As we move along the roped path, we stop at the next wooden sign, which shows us our first line of text. It's a bit long, but short enough to remember using our First Letter Method:

Don't stop letting yourself not memorize the words in this sentence!

What kind of a silly sentence is that? It really has me scratching my head. It's like they made it long and confusing on purpose, just to make it hard for us.

Doesn't matter. The First Letter Method can crack this, no problem.

All right, here are the steps:

◯ **Read** the sentence **in your mind** once or twice.

◯ **Read** it once or twice **out loud**.

◯ Here's where it gets wacky … **Write down** all the **first letters** of each word (including capital letters, lowercase letters, and any punctuation). In this example, that's: D s l y n m t w i t s !

◯ Once you've written it down, **read** from this **first-letter-only** version of the sentence, filling in the complete words as you go. Nine times out of ten, you'll be able to read the sentence perfectly, even though you can only see the first letter of each word. (It's okay to glance back at the original in case you aren't sure of a word.) Read the sentence like this once or twice.

◯ Now for the final magic. Close your eyes and try to **recite it from memory**. It will be there, completely memorized. Try it. It's there, isn't it?

Isn't that absolutely befuddling and amazing at the same time? How did our memory just do that? What always amazes me the most is how our brain can fill in all the words just by seeing the first letter of each word. It just goes to show that if we pay attention, our brain can do some really powerful things!

Let's move on.

If you've ever had to memorize text by rote memorization, you know that it can be done that way . . . eventually. Sometimes, though, that process can take hours, or even days. At a certain point, you'll probably get it. And when the time comes to deliver it, you've got a pretty good shot at nailing it—unless you get nervous, or you suddenly feel tired, or you just get distracted for a moment and in that moment you lose your place, you lose the whole thing, and you wonder if you're losing your mind. AHHHH!

I feel your pain. I've had memory mistakes, too, and they are so embarrassing—especially in front of a bunch of people. When it comes to memorizing a large passage of text, there are two approaches: One is *idea-for-idea* and the other is *word-for-word*.

The *idea-for-idea* approach is when you need to memorize some text, but you don't necessarily need to know every single word, just the basic idea. This works well for a presentation or speech you need to give where you need to make sure you talk about a few things, but you can make up a lot of words around it as you go. Basically, all you need to memorize are the *ideas*. This approach isn't too hard. Just come up with a picture for each general idea or topic you want to talk about (**SEE** it!), then **LINK** it (I would suggest using a memory palace), then **GO!**

Sometimes memorizing the key ideas isn't good enough—you have to get each word exactly right, like a poem, quote, or a speech you'd like to recite word for word. What good would reciting any of those things be if you skipped a bunch of words at a time? No one would ever want to hear that!

The best way to memorize word for word is to use a memory palace to **LINK** (it's the safest and most secure, in my opinion), and to put a few words at a time on each anchor. Now, a lot of the time you'll come across words that are really simple—almost *too* simple—to memorize. Words like *and* or *or* or *the* or *that*, just to name a few. What I like to do for a lot of those common "filler" words is to have preset images. For example, I think of a circle for *and* and a square for *or*. The images can be anything; I just happened to choose those images for those words and stuck with them. (See the Appendix for a longer list of some of my images for these kinds of words.)

We continue climbing up, dodging crevasse after crevasse and avoiding all the massive ice towers. While dangerous, this part of the climb is turning out to actually be pretty fun with lots of interesting zigs and zags. After a few hours, we start to see the top, and after this we'll be in the cwm. But first, another sign! I'm guessing these are the next few lines of text we'll have to memorize before we can advance! The sign reads:

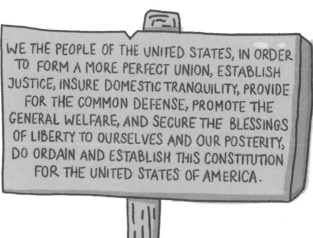

WE THE PEOPLE OF THE UNITED STATES, IN ORDER TO FORM A MORE PERFECT UNION, ESTABLISH JUSTICE, INSURE DOMESTIC TRANQUILITY, PROVIDE FOR THE COMMON DEFENSE, PROMOTE THE GENERAL WELFARE, AND SECURE THE BLESSINGS OF LIBERTY TO OURSELVES AND OUR POSTERITY, DO ORDAIN AND ESTABLISH THIS CONSTITUTION FOR THE UNITED STATES OF AMERICA.

I'll help get you started. Before we begin, we'll need to choose a memory palace to store it all. To make things more fun, I'm going to use a memory palace that is a tad different than what you might expect (just to give you an extra example of how creative you can be with your memory palace choices). I'm going to use a U.S. map for this one since it has to do with U.S. history. (It's the preamble to the U.S. Constitution, in case you didn't know!) The anchor points along our path will be the big cities around the country! The path will be: starting in Miami and moving up the East Coast to Washington, D.C., then Philadelphia, New York, and Boston; heading west toward Chicago, Denver, and San Francisco; and finally, down to L.A. (You can add as many cities as you like—these are just a few to get you started.) Since a city name in itself isn't super memorable, the thing we'll use to attach our images to will be some memorable thing about each city:

Miami	→	Beach
D.C.	→	White House
Philadelphia	→	Liberty Bell
New York	→	Empire State Building
Boston	→	Boston Harbor
Chicago	→	Sears Tower
Denver	→	Rocky Mountains
San Francisco	→	Golden Gate Bridge
Los Angeles	→	Hollywood Sign
San Diego	→	Surfing waves

Before you start storing the text in your memory palace, try reading the whole thing through. When doing that, really try to be *in* the text. As you read the words, picture them playing out in your mind, and as you see them, try to feel the emotion of each line. Try to understand and feel its meaning. After reading it once, read it again. This time, pay more attention to the structure of the text, how it flows, and if it rhymes. This will give you a head start on knowing a lot about the text when it comes time to memorize it.

In this particular text, it's one really long sentence, so let's split it up. Here's how I'd break it down:

NOTE TO READER

There's no right or wrong way to split up the sentences of a text or poem. I like to split them in half, but not always. If a sentence is short, I'll just take the whole thing as one image. If a sentence is long, I might even split it in three or four pieces. It all depends. The important thing here is to be flexible and do what feels good to you.

● **"We the People of the United States,"** . . .

We're standing in Miami on the beach (our first anchor point) and we need to picture this short phrase happening there. It's pretty self-explanatory, but I would picture a group of people on the beach, pointing to themselves ("we") as if they were "the People of the United States." If you want to remember "we" better, maybe imagine everyone sliding down a fun slide, screaming, "Weeeeeee!"

● **"in Order to form a more perfect Union,"** . . .

Now you're in D.C., in front of the White House. I might imagine a restaurant menu out front—one that I dive into as I order food. As I dive in, I receive two forms ("to form") that I must fill out for the United States to become "a more perfect Union."

● "establish Justice," . . .

Next up, you're in Philadelphia, checking out the Liberty Bell. I'm going to imagine a table (table = "es-table-ish") inside the bell. At that table is a judge, slamming her gavel down in the name of JUSTICE!

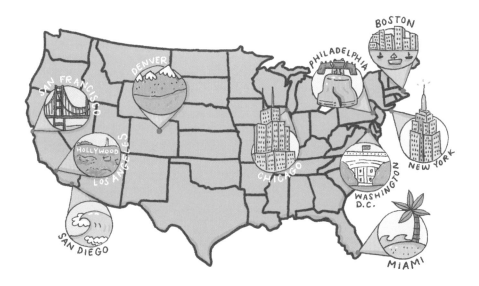

What about punctuation? There are a few commas, and one period, scattered throughout the paragraph. Well, if you're reciting the text out loud, punctuation doesn't really matter because you don't *say* the punctuation. But if you have to write it down perfectly, you'll need to know it. I would come up with some premade images for those punctuation marks and then add them to your image. (I have some you can use, in the Appendix.)

This is your challenge now! I want you to try and do the rest of this text on your own. I know you can do it! Make sure to try and recite it for a friend or family member when you're done. They will be impressed! It's an incredible line from one of the most memorable texts in U.S. history. (Have a look at the Appendix afterward, to see how I would have memorized the remaining images.)

Into the Equation Cwm we go. The dangerously crevassed section of the climb is over and now we see a gentle slope before us, sandwiched in between two mountainsides, with the summit of Foreverest in front of us, in full view. We slog on up the snowy path for an hour or so before reaching our next sign:

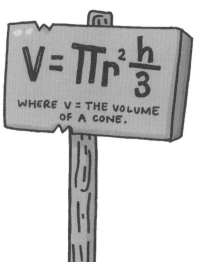

$$V = \pi r^2 \frac{h}{3}$$

WHERE V = THE VOLUME OF A CONE.

Welcome to the Equation Cwm, the second of three challenging features on the mountain. You will have to memorize the following math equation, filled with numbers and symbols—some you may not ever have seen before! Memorize them and continue . . . if you dare!

$V = \pi r^2\, h/3$

Where V is the volume of a cone.

Okay, you can do this! Numbers we know how to come up with images for, equations we know how to memorize (think back to those *word* equations we memorized in chapter 4), but some of these random letters or symbols . . . Eh, maybe not so sure?

By now you probably have a good idea of what I'm going to suggest in how to memorize those symbols and how to keep it all together. **SEE-LINK-GO!** To **LINK** it all together I'll use what I learned in chapter 4: come up with a picture for the left side, a picture for the right side, then connect them. For any letters I see, if I know what it stands for, I'll try to come up with a picture related to that meaning. If it's a symbol, I may have to premake some images for those.

● $V = \pi r^2 h/3$

The left-hand side is the easiest, since it's just the letter V. We know it stands for "volume of a cone." If I'm familiar with math and volume, I know volume has to do with how much space a three-dimensional object takes up. But let's say I don't. Volume might make me think of *loudness*. I could picture turning a cone like a volume knob on a stereo to make the music louder!

For the right-hand side, we have a lot going on. Let's move from left to right, and string all the pieces together in a mini Story Method story.

- π = there's the symbol for pi again! (Can you remember the twenty-one digits we memorized back in the last chapter?) I'll think of a pizza **PIE** for this one.

- r^2 = r stands for radius, which is the length from the center of a circle to its edge. Radius makes me think of RADIO. Since it's raised to the second power, or squared, we can imagine this **RADIO** is **SQUARED**, or in the shape of a square.

- **h** = h stands for height, as in the height of the cone from base to tip. Height reminds me of measuring how **TALL** something is.

- **/** = this means divide. To me it looks like a samurai SWORD slicing through something. **SCHLINK**!

- **3** = A number! Easy! We can use our Number-Shape or Rhyme System from the last chapter. I'm going to use a shape. How about that **BUTTERFLY**?

So let's make our story for the RHS: There's this pizza PIE listening to a SQUARE RADIO. Then a samurai walks in and demands to measure the HEIGHT of the pizza, but he gets angry when the pizza refuses, so he takes out his SWORD and slices it into pieces small enough a BUTTERFLY could eat!

Next, let's connect it to the other side of the equation. Imagine right *on* that radio, the VOLUME knob is cone-shaped!

NOTE TO READER

Memorizing something and understanding something isn't always the same thing. Remember, all the techniques I'm showing you are designed to help you memorize faster; to get information in your brain faster. Not necessarily to understand it immediately. Once you've memorized it, though, you can take all the time you want to understand the information, since it's already in your head.

Some people might argue that memorization is not learning, but I disagree. Memorization is a step in the learning process, and a very important one at that!

See if you can close your eyes and say the equation we just learned, without looking. Once you've done that, see if you can try this same process on some equations you need to know for your next math test!

That wasn't too hard, was it? Next up, the Password Wall! After learning the equation and plodding on for a few more hours, we finally reach the base of the wall. We look up to see a very steep route indeed, and all on very slippery ice. We'll have to make sure we use our crampons and ice axes for this section! Looking more carefully, we can make out eight different ice bolt anchors for us to pass through with our ropes. That means there will probably be eight symbol characters for the password we need to memorize. The sign at the base of the face reads:

WELCOME TO THE PASSWORD WALL, THE LAST OF THE THREE CHALLENGING FEATURES ON THE MOUNTAIN. YOU WILL HAVE TO MEMORIZE A VERY DIFFICULT PASSWORD, WITH LOTS OF SYMBOLS, LETTERS, AND CHARACTERS. MEMORIZE IT AND CONTINUE ON . . . TO THE SUMMIT OF MOUNT FOREVEREST!

Since we're roped up, we'll have to move through this section close together. I'll climb and clip in with my rope to each anchor first, then secure you as you climb up after me, until you're safely clipped in as well. Then you can memorize the character, and then we'll move on to the next anchor. Ready?

As we clip in and out, up and up, we collect all the characters as we go. We see the following:

➡ @

For symbols like these, I would just come up with a quick image for what it reminds me of. This reminds me of an email address, because all email addresses have one! So let's imagine EMAIL.

➡ L

Aha! The letter *L*. Like we did in the previous equation, we can come up with a word starting with that letter. Maybe LAMBORGHINI? The snazziest car ever made! Since it's a capital letter, make your Lamborghini HUGE. (Anything big will help us remember it was a big letter, not a small one.)

Two numbers! Easy peasy! Just use the Major System. 65 could translate to SHELL or JAIL. Let's use JAIL (6 = SH or J; 5 = L).

➡ !

Another symbol. It looks like a BASEBALL BAT.

➡ ~

This one looks like a MUSTACHE.

Think of your PA; your dad, miniature in size (because of the lowercase letters).

%

For this symbol, it looks like someone SLASHING a SNOWMAN right IN HALF. The two circles are the snowman halves and the slash is the knife cutting through.

 X

A lowercase *x*. I'll go with X-RAY (a small, itty-bitty one).

Next, **LINK** it all together using **THE STORY METHOD** (since it's the quickest and requires the least prep).

The last step, once you've put all these symbols together, is to attach it to what the password is for. This is the most important part. If you can remember the password, that's great and everything. But what use is it if you can't remember what it was used for? Was it for your email? YouTube? Instagram? Your bank account? Uh-oh!

Try and come up with your own story to bring it all together! Check the Appendix to see my story for some guidance.

Think of what the password accesses. Let's say for this example, it's the password for your online bank account. (If you don't have a bank account yet, maybe ask your parents to open one for you and start saving!) Now attach an image of a bank—maybe picture a huge vault filled with coins and dollar bills, miles high!—to the story you made up for the password.

Got it? Good!

Now we're at the top of the face. Great climbing! PHEW! I'm exhausted from all this climbing, aren't you? With the last few hundred feet to walk up, we start to see a figure in the distance. Could it be . . . the Memory Thief?

Closer and closer we get, and the worse the weather becomes. Wind and snow start whipping at our faces. It's hard to see anything until, finally, it's so blizzardy that we can't even see a few feet in front of us.

We carry on, step after careful step. Each one is difficult and painful, needing a few breaths in between each so we can gather strength. The high altitude is taking its toll on our breathing, but we're at the heights where jumbo jets fly, so that's not a surprise!

"MWA-HAHAHAHA!" we hear suddenly in front of us. "IT IS I, THE MEMORY THIEF. YOU ARE FOOLS TO HAVE COME HERE. NO ONE CAN DEFEAT ME, FOR I CAN STEAL YOUR MEMORIES IN AN INSTANT."

In a quick moment, the blizzard disperses, and we now see the monster before us. He's gigantic—towering twenty feet tall—and heavy-set, covered in slimy green skin with white spots all over his belly. With three bulging eyeballs, two jagged horns on his head, massive claws, and sharp fangs, this Memory Thief is no joke! He is one scary monster.

But you know what to do, young memory master! Hit him first with those lines of text!

Can you recall the first stand-alone sentence and then the parts of the U.S. Constitution Preamble that you memorized? Hurry, try it!

You recite the line and instantly the Memory Thief falls to one knee, growling in agony. He slashes out with his arms wildly, narrowly missing the both of us as we jump aside.

"ARGHHHH! WHAT HAVE YOU DONE TO ME?! MY EARS! MY HEAD! MY EYES! WHY DO THEY HURT SO MUCH! WAS THAT LINE OF TEXT FROM MEMORY? I HATE RECITED TEXT!"

After being fazed for a few moments, he regains his strength, stands up, and charges forward with the speed of an accelerating monster truck.

Quick! Hit him with that equation you learned!

Can you recall the equation we just learned? Fast, try and say it out loud from memory!

You recite the equation perfectly and the Memory Thief trips and tumbles partway down the side of the mountain, hitting a few rocks along the way. He finally comes to a stop, having barely caught himself on the edge of a small overhang using one of his claws.

"OOFF! OUCH! ARGH! MY LEGS! MY ARMS! EVERYTHING HURTS! I HATE EQUATIONS! ESPECIALLY FROM MEMORY!"

He shakes it off, pulls himself up, and vaults into the air, landing with a thunderous BOOM right in front of us on the summit. He's so close to us now we can smell his hot, foul, beastly breath.

"THIS IS WHERE I FINISH YOU TWO OFF! ENOUGH OF THIS! YOU CANNOT DEFEAT ME! I WILL TAKE OVER ALL THE MEMORIES IN THE WORLD, YOURS INCLUDED!"

Last but not least, hit him with the final password! This should do him in.

Think of the password you just memorized. Recall it! Now!

As you say the last few characters of the password, we notice the Memory Thief start to shake uncontrollably. He grabs his head, writhing in pain, screaming out loud, "ARGHHHHHH! NOOOOOO! THIS CAN'T BE!"

First his arms, then his legs, limb by limb, start to crumble away. The rest of his body falls to the ground, shaking violently. Then, POOF! He's gone. A few wisps of dust float up into the air, but otherwise there's no trace left of him at all. The Memory Thief is no more. Waves of clouds shoot out from the summit of the mountain, spreading in all directions, blanketing the lands below. That must be the memories being restored to the rest of the planet!

I can't believe it, you did it! I was there to help you only a bit, but no thanks to my failing memory . . . which, hey . . . now that I think of it, it's back in full force! I remember everything now: the river, the forest, the desert, pirates, the palace, all of it, and in so much detail. It's all thanks to you and your amazing memory skills and perseverance. I knew I could count on you when you decided to join me many adventures ago!

The weather has completely cleared now, revealing the glorious views from so high up in the sky. We are at such a lofty altitude, we can even see the curve of the earth! All that's left to do now is to take in these amazing sights from the summit and then start our journey back home, knowing that we've restored the memory of everyone on the planet. Ah, what a feeling!

NOTE TO READER

Well done! With your memory training complete, you can now go out into the world and use your memory for whatever you want. I hope you use it! Memory is one of the most useful life skills you can ever learn. What's even better is that not a lot of people know these skills. So just by reading this book, you have instantly become smarter than the average person—you've literally got your own superpower now: an incredible memory. That's a pretty cool feeling, isn't it?

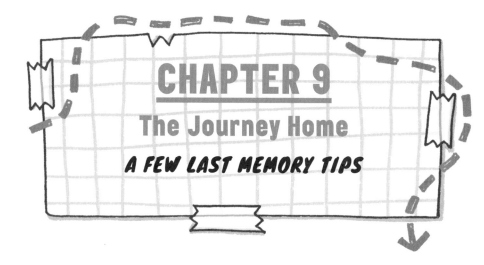

CHAPTER 9

The Journey Home

A FEW LAST MEMORY TIPS

With the Memory Thief defeated, and after having celebrated a bit on the summit of Mount Foreverest (it *is* the tallest place on earth, after all, why not celebrate?), you realize something. The mind tools you brought along with you? They were with you all along. You already had the power of those tools within you—you already had memory superpowers. It was just a matter of someone showing you how to use them correctly. Hopefully, with my help, you've been able to do that.

As we make our way back home, let me give you a few parting tips to round out your new memory powers.

First, and most important, know that all I've taught you is a way to put things in your memory *quickly*. I can't stress that enough. That's all these techniques do. Now, that doesn't make them any less important. I just want you to understand what they truly are. Once you understand that, you can begin to use these techniques for some real powerful memorizing for the long-term.

Which brings me to my next point. To keep all these things you want to memorize in your head *forever*, you'll need to do something that isn't always enjoyable. But you must. And that is: review.

Ugh! I know. You must be thinking, *Review, Nelson? Really? After all that, you're going to tell me I need to study and review?*

Sadly, yes. Hey, I didn't design the human brain; that's just how it works. Nothing you or I can do to change that. Even without the Memory Thief, our brains were designed to forget things over time. That's why when you study only once, it usually isn't enough to remember something for a long time. But with memory techniques, the nice thing is, they organize all the information you've memorized and give you easy access to review them in your mind, whenever you want. And a lot of the time when I memorize something, I only have to look at it once. I **SEE-LINK-GO!** it, get it into my memory, and then if I want to keep it for a long time, I just mentally review it from time to time. (Review really only means "think about it," if you've memorized it well using the techniques covered in this book. Thinking isn't hard, right?)

So, in short:

If you want to remember something forever, keep reviewing it.

NOTE TO READER

How many times should you review? How often? These are common questions I get and there isn't a precise answer; everyone is different. In general, review a lot at the beginning when you first learn something, then cut back over time (but still review it from time to time). The time between review sessions almost doubles each time. That could look something like this: You learn the information, immediately review it, review it one hour later, review before bed, review the next morning, then review one day after that, then a few days after that, then a week later, then a week after that, then two weeks, then a month, then six months, then a year. By that point (or maybe even sooner; as I mentioned before, it depends on the person), you should have it in your long-term memory, and it will be there forever.

Let's talk about studying. As a student, you probably have to study for a lot of things. And you and I both know that studying and reviewing can feel boring at times. This can sometimes cause me to procrastinate and dread sitting down and studying, which sometimes ends up with me not studying at all (or studying very little).

Turn off or put away all nearby distractions—no social media, TV, or books—and study, completely focused, for a chunk of time that you decide feels right. No cheating! Once the time is up, take a five-minute break to do whatever fun thing you want to do. Check your email, play a game on your phone, text your friends, whatever! But only for five minutes, okay? Then set the timer for another session and get back to studying. Then take another break when it's over. You can repeat this for as long as you like, but I suggest that you take one longer break (fifteen minutes is good) after about a full hour of studying, just to break things up a bit more.

Next, I can't remind you enough to *pay attention*. A lot of memory mistakes happen because you stopped paying attention. If you work on *one* thing at a time and try to be more present, in the moment, you'll find that your memory will oftentimes improve on its own. Here are some quick examples of things we forget a lot, that can be fixed with a quick *pay attention* punch in the face!

Remembering names

We went over this in chapter 3, but I'll remind you here again. If you tell yourself, in your mind, "I want to remember this person's name" as you're meeting them, you'll pay better attention and be more likely to remember the name.

● Remembering where you put things

We all do this; misplacing items around our house. Things like keys, our homework folder, even our backpacks. Here's a quick tip if you forget things like this a lot. When you place the item down, remember to do a funny action or make a funny sound out loud—something totally bizarre that no one in the universe has ever said or done. Go ahead, try it! It's fun! Later, when you're trying to remember where you placed it, you'll remember the weird thing you did or said and remember where it is! Ta-da!

• BONUS TIP: If you're prone to forgetting stuff like this, try to plan for your future self. That means, try to place things in the same spot all the time so that future you doesn't even need to think about it. The item you're looking for is always in the same place. That's easy, isn't it?

● Remembering if you did something already

Have you ever been in the shower and washed your hair, only to forget a few minutes later that you did and then you washed your hair all over again? You can also use the previous technique to help you remember something you already did. Just make sure to make a strange action or noise once you complete the thing.

TO DO:
☑ CLEAN
☐ HOME-
   WORK
☐ SOCCER

● Remembering things you need to do in the morning

Sometimes you're in bed and suddenly think of something you need to do in the morning. You don't want to get out of bed and write it down, so instead what you can do is a fun little technique called the Throw the Pen Method. Grab something on your bedside table—a pen or any object that's there—and toss it on the floor. Make sure to toss it in an area where your future morning self will notice it. And then think of an image for the thing you need to do in the morning and **LINK** it to the pen (or item) that you threw on the floor. It's like an instant anchor point!

● Remembering why you walked into a room

Do you walk into a room and suddenly forget what you're doing there? Me too! Simple solution? Go back into the previous room you were in. That usually will trigger the memory of what your purpose was in the other room. For some reason, walking through doorways can make us forget things, so before you pass through one, double-check your memory.

● How to be mindful

Memory is all about being mindful and present. In other words, remembering to remember. Practicing these memory techniques will help you get better at this, but a quick way to bring yourself into the moment is to ask yourself questions about what is happening around you *right* now, at *this* moment. Try to observe as much around you as you can and use all your senses!

Last but not least, there are a few things you can do *outside* of memory techniques to make your brain sharper. Here are a few things to keep in mind as you continue on your personal journey of being a cool memory master:

 GET SOME SLEEP! Sleep is a really important part of having a sharp brain. Without it, you'll feel groggy, moody, and unable to focus easily. If you can force yourself to get a good night's rest each night, you'll be doing your brain a favor. Try getting to bed on time every night and keep distractions to a minimum. No phones in bed! Bed is for sleeping! Try to get at least eight hours of sleep a night.

 EAT RIGHT Believe it or not, eating the right foods can change your brain. Lots of sugary foods can harm your brain, so try to stick to healthy brain foods like fish, green leafy veggies, almonds, and blueberries.

 EXERCISE Stay active! The brain needs a lot of blood pumping into it from around your body. Exercising or staying active helps keep blood flow to the brain nice and smooth. The more active you are, the sharper you'll feel your brain is.

 TAKE IT EASY Hey, relax! There's no need to stress. It's actually bad for your brain. Stress can sometimes be hard to control—maybe you have too much homework or your parents are asking a lot from you—but you can (and should) always take a step back, look at everything, and tell yourself: Hey! This is my life! I'm enjoying it! I'm happy and lucky to be alive. Just relax, be happy, no need to stress.

That's that! I can't think of anything more to tell you. This book has taken you through all of it! Well, everything *I* know, at least. It's been an absolute pleasure adventuring with you. Hopefully we can do it again sometime!

Oh, one more thing, before I forget . . . I . . . uh . . . oh wait, I must have forgotten it!

APPENDIX

VISIT MEMORYSUPERPOWERS.COM TO LEARN
- ALL 45 U.S. PRESIDENTS
- ALL U.S. STATES AND CAPITALS
- CAPITALS OF ALL 195 COUNTRIES
- THE ENTIRE PERIODIC TABLE
- TIMES TABLES

● ANSWERS

CHAPTER 3, PAGE 47:

- **Brian**—a brain

- **Sarah**—a cheerleader with pom-poms going, "RAH-RAH-RAH!"

- **Ryan**—a frying pan

- **David**—a dove

- **Bridgette**—a bridge

PAGE 58:

- **Trish:** For Trish, I think of someone saying, "Trish or Treat!" (Sounds similar to "trick," doesn't it?) Since she's got thick eyebrows, I would picture someone grabbing her eyebrows after saying, "Trish or treat," like they were a bunch of candies.

- **William:** For William, I think of a written will—a really old, long scroll-of-a-document. It's coming out of his mustache, of course!

- **Mary:** Mary sounds like *marry*. I'm going to imagine a big marriage procession happening all over her big smile.

CHAPTER 4, PAGE 67:

- **Indignant**—expressing strong displeasure at something offensive.
  For the LHS I would think of "dig-ant." For the RHS, let's try to make that simpler. Maybe "really not liking something" is good enough. So let's imagine digging up a bunch of ants and that they smell so bad that you start complaining really loudly about how much you don't like it: "AWWW YUCK, THIS IS SO GROSS! I HATE THIS!"

- **Teem**—to abound or swarm; be prolific or fertile.
Teem sounds like *team*. Again, I'm going to make the definition easier. It's basically saying something like "there's a lot of something." Let's imagine you're playing on a team (whatever sport you like) and there are hundreds of players on your team. How annoying! Your team is teeming with players!

- **Protrude**—to thrust forward.
Protrude sounds like a *pro* who is *rude*. Maybe he's a professional rude person? "Thrust forward" is basically making something go forward really quickly. Imagine this pro-rude person being so rude that he approaches you really fast. He thrusts forward at you.

PAGE 70:

- ***Cerf-volant*** (pronounced "surf-vol-aunt")—kite
"Surf-vol-aunt" is almost good enough for our picture, but what's a vol? Maybe we can replace it with "bowl"? Close enough. So imagine surfing on a bowl with your aunt and as you guys are surfing, a kite comes from out of nowhere and hits you both in the face. Ouch!

- ***Souris*** (pronounced "sue-ree")—mouse
Imagine suing a mouse and you're reeeeeeally happy about it. Sue-reeeeee that mouse!

- **Débile** (pronounced "deh-beel")—silly, dumb
  Deh-beel sounds a bit like *the-peel*. Imagine
  slipping on THE banana PEEL that's on the
  ground and how silly and dumb you would look
  like flying in the air and landing on your butt.

PAGE 79:

- **Belgium—Brussels**
  - Belgium reminds me of a BELL working out at
    the GYM. Brussels makes me think of BRUSSEL
    sprouts. Imagine a bell going to work out at
    the gym and eating tons of brussel sprouts.

- **Chile—Santiago**
  - This one is quick and easy. Think of SANTA
    CLAUS being CHILLY. Maybe he took off his
    big coat and is only in a t-shirt at the North
    Pole. (Chilly = Chile, Santiago = Santa).

- **Finland—Helsinki**
  - Imagine a land where there are only fins, nothing
    else (that's FINLAND). Think of how you
    might sink into the ground there, so you scream
    for help (HELP-SINKING! = Helsinki).

- **Namibia—Windhoek**
  - Imagine NAMING a BABY (Name-baby = Namibia) and as you do that, the WIND blows HOOKS all around you (Wind-hook = Windhoek). So maybe that inspires you to name your kid Windhoek.

- **Nepal—Kathmandu**
  - Nepal rhymes with PIMPLE. Kathmandu sounds like CAT-MAN-DO (a CAT and a MAN DOing something). What if what the cat and the man were doing, was popping big old nasty pimples. Ew!

CHAPTER 5, PAGE 103:

⇒ Some Extra Alphabet Peg Lists

Here are two examples of some different Alphabet Peg Lists. I have one where the letter represents the first letter of the alphabet letter, while the other one is based on a rhyming scheme. Use whichever suits your fancy, or customize it so it works with your own associations. Using categories like we did in chapter 5 with all the animals is another option. You can use foods, sports, cartoon characters, whatever!

Starting *with* the letter, here is just a generic non-themed peg list:

A—Apple	J—Jar	S—Sock
B—Bat	K—Kite	T—Toy
C—Car	L—Log	U—Umbrella
D—Door	M—Man	V—Vane
E—Elephant	N—Nut	W—Wig
F—Fish	O—Owl	X—X-ray
G—Grass	P—Pig	Y—Yak
H—House	Q—Quill	Z—Zoo
I—Ice cream	R—Rock	

Here is a peg list where the image *sounds* like the letter:

A—Hay	J—Jay	S—Sass
B—Bee	K—Key	T—Tea
C—See	L—Elbow	U—Ewe
D—Deed	M—Hem	V—Veal
E—Eve	N—Hen	W—Double you
F—Effort	O—Hoe	X—Ax
G—Jeep	P—Pea	Y—Wire
H—Age	Q—Cue	Z—Zebra
I—Eye	R—Oar	

Here's a fun food category peg list:

A—Apple	**J**—Jelly	**S**—Sausage
B—Banana	**K**—Kit-Kat	**T**—Toast
C—Carrot	**L**—Lemon	**U**—Udon noodles
D—Date	**M**—Macaroni	**V**—Vinegar
E—Eggplant	**N**—Nuts	**W**—Wheat
F—French fry	**O**—Oreo	**X**—Xtra spicy sauce
G—Green bean	**P**—Pumpkin	(X is a tough one!)
H—Honey	**Q**—Quiche	**Y**—Yogurt
I—Ice cream	**R**—Rice	**Z**—Zucchini

Here's a sports-themed category peg list:

A—Archery	**H**—Hoop	**O**—Obstacle
B—Baseball bat	(basketball	course
C—Cleat	hoop)	**P**—Ping-pong ball
D—Dumbell	**I**—Ice skate	**Q**—Quidditch
E—Equestrian	**J**—Javelin	broomstick
(horse riding)	**K**—Kettlebell	**R**—Racket
F—Football	**L**—Lacrosse stick	**S**—Soccer ball
G—Goal (soccer	**M**—Mouthpiece	**T**—Tennis ball
goal)	**N**—Net	

U—Ultimate frisbee	W—Wakeboard	Z—Ziplining
V—Volleyball	X—Xtreme skating	
	Y—Yacht sailing	

CHAPTER 7, PAGE 143:

- **68**—SHAVE or JIFF

- **71**—CAT or KIT

- **18**—TAFFY or TOUGH

- **RAT**—41

- **PUKE**—97

- **SPELL**—095

- **SPAGHETTI**—0971

PAGE 149:

- **1905**—Einstein writes physics paper
  I turned 19-05 into DIP-SAIL. So I imagined DIPping a SAIL into Einstein's crazy white scientist hair as he is writing his famous paper on special relativity.

- **1885—First car is built**
  18-85 becomes TAFFY-FALL. That's going to be some TAFFY FALLing onto the very first car being built. Oh no! That car is now destroyed and covered in TAFFY.

- **1953—First Mount Everest summit**
  19-53 becomes DAB-LLAMA. Think of a LLAMA reaching the summit of Mount Everest and DABbing in celebration.

- **2007—First iPhone released**
  20-07 becomes NOSE-SACK. Imagine you have a NOSE SACK (a SACK hanging from your NOSE) and you're just filling it up with all the first iPhones that are available so you can take them around selling them to people.

PAGE 151:

14 = TIRE	**35** = MULE	**79** = CAPE
15 = DOLL	**89** = FIB	**32** = MOON
92 = PEN	(FIB is a another	**38** = MOVIE
65 = JELLO	word for "lie")	**46** = RASH

• Using **THE STORY METHOD,** my story I had was:
A **TIRE** rolling down the street that hits a **DOLL**
holding a **PEN**. The **PEN** flies out of her hand into
some green, jiggly **JELLO**, which is sitting on the
back of **MULE**. This **MULE** tells a **FIB** (a lie) and
then covers himself up with a **CAPE**. The **MOON**
shines down on his **CAPE**, which projects a **MOVIE**
on it so powerfully that it causes a **RASH**.

Phew! All done! Was my story similar to yours in any way?

PAGE 154:

➡ Major System Images for 00–99:

• **00**—sauce	• **06**—switch	• **12**—tin
• **01**—seed	• **07**—sky	• **13**—tomb
• **02**—sun	• **08**—sofa	• **14**—tire
• **03**—sumo	• **09**—soap	• **15**—doll
• **04**—sore	• **10**—toes	• **16**—dish
• **05**—soil	• **11**—tot	• **17**—tack

- **18**—tough
- **19**—tub
- **20**—nose
- **21**—net
- **22**—nun
- **23**—nom
- **24**—Nero
- **25**—nail
- **26**—nacho
- **27**—knock
- **28**—knife
- **29**—knob
- **30**—mouse
- **31**—mat

- **32**—moon
- **33**—mom
- **34**—mayor
- **35**—mule
- **36**—match
- **37**—mug
- **38**—movie
- **39**—map
- **40**—rice
- **41**—rat
- **42**—rain
- **43**—rum
- **44**—rower
- **45**—rail

- **46**—rash
- **47**—rag
- **48**—roof
- **49**—rope
- **50**—lace
- **51**—lid
- **52**—lion
- **53**—lime
- **54**—lawyer
- **55**—lily
- **56**—leech
- **57**—leg
- **58**—lava
- **59**—lip

60—shoes	**74**—car	**88**—high-five
61—cheetah	**75**—coal	**89**—fib
62—chin	**76**—cage	**90**—boss
63—gem	**77**—cake	**91**—bat
64—jar	**78**—cave	**92**—pen
65—Jell-O	**79**—cape	**93**—bum
66—judge	**80**—fizzy	**94**—bear
67—chick	**81**—video	**95**—bell
68—shave	**82**—phone	**96**—beach
69—ship	**83**—foam	**97**—book
70—case	**84**—fairy	**98**—beef
71—cat	**85**—foil	**99**—pipe
72—coin	**86**—fish	
73—comb	**87**—fig	

CHAPTER 8, PAGE 163:

➤ Filler Words Images for Poems and Texts

Here are words that will often come up in text or poem memorization. These words alone don't really mean much, so they can be tricky when trying to infuse them with a fun, memorable picture. Here are just a few of the common ones. The rest, I'll just improvise on the fly (as can you).

- **AND** = circle
- **OR** = square
- **OF** = off switch
- **THIS** = hiss
- **THAT** = hat
- **I** = eye
- **BUT** = butt

- **AS** = donkey
- **SO** = sew
- **THEN** = hen
- **THING** = hinge
- **IT** = hit
- **IF** = cliff

PAGE 167:

➤ Images for Punctuation Marks and Characters

Here are some images I have for remembering characters and punctuation marks. Most of these come from what I feel is right; or what I think the character looks like. Notice that all of them are actions—it's more memorable that way. You can also use some of these images for characters you might need to memorize in a password.

. = POKING SOMETHING

, = FALLING DOWN

? = HOOKING SOMETHING

! = ELECTRIFYING SOMETHING

: = ZAPPING

; = MOPPING

= POUNDING SOMETHING

$ = SLITHERING AROUND

& = DRIVING

PAGE 168:

- **"insure domestic Tranquility,"** ...
  In New York, at the Empire State Building.
  I would picture the massive building being
  INSURED and a DOME being STUCK to it via
  a TRANQUILIZER dart (insure-dome-stick-
  tranquilizer = insure domestic Tranquility).

- **"Provide for the common defense,"** ...
  In the middle of the Boston Harbor, imagine a big ship
  docked there, PROVIDING FOUR (for) different
  COMMON DEFENSES (maybe imagine FOUR
  basketball players playing COMMON DEFENSE).
  To help you remember "COMMON," maybe imagine
  the players are saying, "Come on!" egging you on.

- **"Promote the general Welfare,"** ...
  At the Sears Tower in Chicago, one of the tallest,
  most iconic buildings in the country, I'll imagine
  a guy standing outside, PROMOTING a military
  GENERAL (all decked out in his military gear)
  whose name happens to be WELFARE.

- **"And secure the Blessings of Liberty"** ...
  In the Rocky Mountains, I would imagine SECURING
  a sneeze (BLESS YOU = Blessings). Maybe to
  secure something, you imagine attaching a lock to

your nose and throwing away the key. You sneeze (BLESS YOU) and the Statue of LIBERTY flies out and lands on the mountainside. Icky!

- **"To ourselves and our Posterity,"** ...
Almost there! At the Golden Gate Bridge, imagine TWO of YOURSELF (To ourselves) and an HOUR (our) glass where POST-IT notes are falling through instead of sand (POST-IT = Posterity).

- **"Do ordain and establish this Constitution for the United States of America."**
Finally, we're in Los Angeles, at the Hollywood Sign. Imagine you have a hair-DO that gets ruined by the RAIN (RAIN = ordain) and that you STAB (e-stab-lish) the document that is the CONSTITUTION FOR THE UNITED STATES OF AMERICA!

PAGE 174:

You're sitting there, writing an EMAIL, when all of a sudden, a BIG LAMBORGHINI zips by. The police pull the driver over and take him to JAIL, where he is given a BASEBALL BAT. He has to disguise himself so no one recognizes him, so he wears a MUSTACHE and surprisingly looks a lot like your mini-PA. He walks over to a SNOWMAN and CUTS IT IN HALF with the bat. The snowman has to then get a tiny X-RAY to see if he's okay. (He's not, he was just sliced in half!)

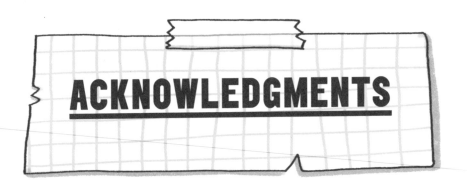

ACKNOWLEDGMENTS

This book has been a dream of mine since my early days of competing in memory competitions. When I started giving speeches and teaching others these techniques, I quickly realized that kids (out of everyone that I would teach) were naturally inclined to think in the way these techniques work—being silly and thinking in funny pictures. Ever since then, I always hoped to write a book for that age group (especially since these techniques aren't taught to them in school). And now here we are!

Thanks to my loving wife, Leah, for putting up with me during all the late night writing sessions.

This book wouldn't exist without my agent, Jim Levine. We started with just the adult book in mind, but suddenly a kids book was on the table as well. Amazing.

A huge thanks to the team at Abrams who helped edit, work on, design, and promote this book. Specifically David Cashion and Jody Mosley who were the guiding forces behind the tone and direction of the book.

Also a massive thanks to Steph Stilwell for her insanely perfect-for-this-book illustrations. I don't think anyone else could have captured the craziness written in this book like she did.